The Missing Piece: How Traceability Links Recovery Strengthens Software Systems

Mahima

Contents

Part I

Introduction

Introduction

*This chapter introduces this **book**, highlighting the motivation for the research and the objectives of this work, as well as providing an overview of the **book** and of the scientific articles included in this compendium document. Finally, this chapter presents the methodology followed to pursue this research, and states the structure of the document.*

Motivation

Traceability Links Recovery (TLR) is defined as the software engineering task that deals with the identification and comprehension of dependencies and relationships between software artifacts (Oliveto et al. 2010). TLR is an important support activity during development, management, and maintenance of software, since it is helpful for a number of software tasks such as requirement coverage, software reuse, program comprehension, or impact analysis. In addition, TLR is considered as a good practice by numerous major software standards such as CMMI or ISO 15504 (Oliveto et al. 2010). Moreover, research has shown that affordable traceability can be critical to the success of a project (Watkins and Neal 1994), and leads to increased maintainability and reliability of software systems by making it possible to verify and trace non-reliable parts (Ghazarian 2010). Specifically, m ore c omplete t raceability d ecreases t he expected defect rate in developed software (Rempel and Mäder 2017).

Even though all of these factors vouch for TLR, being able to establish and maintain traceability links has proven to be a time consuming, error prone, and person-power intensive task (Oliveto et al. 2010; Zhang et al. 2008). Therefore, TLR has been a subject of investigation for many years within the software engineering community (Gotel and Finkelstein 1994; Spanoudakis and Zisman 2005), and in recent years, it has been attracting more attention, becoming a subject of both fundamental and applied research (Parizi, Lee, and Dabbagh 2014). However, most of the works focus on performing TLR between requirements and code (Rubin and Chechik 2013), and the application of TLR techniques to models in general, and BPMN models in particular, is a topic that has not received enough attention yet.

book Objectives

Based on the context provided in the motivation section, the main goal of this book is to analyze and improve the Traceability Links Recovery process between natural language requirements and BPMN models. To that extent, the following research questions are defined for the book:

RQ1 Is it possible to adapt state-of-the-art Information Retrieval approaches in order to make them available for Traceability Links Recovery between natural language requirements and BPMN models?

RQ2 If so, how can we refine the proposed approaches in order to improve the Traceability Links Recovery process between natural language requirements and BPMN models?

The results of the research carried out to fulfill t he p ursued objectives have been published in several articles, introduced in the following section.

book Overview

Figure 1 presents an overview of the works that we carried out in order to respond to the research questions posed by the book. We started the book by identifying the most novel, state-of-the-art approaches in Trace-ability Links Recovery, and concentrated our initial efforts in transform-ing the approaches towards their application to model-based software artifacts. We successfully leveraged the state-of-the-art approaches and techniques for Traceability Links Recovery between natural language re-quirements and generic conceptual models, publishing the results of the work derived from our initial ideas in a paper for CAiSE Forum '17 (Lapeña, Font, Cetina, and Ó. Pastor 2017).

During the development of our first research ideas, we realized the importance of the role that natural language plays in the Traceability Links Recovery process: the approaches in use determine their outcomes through semantic and linguistic similitude between the artifacts in use, and both the requirements and models are incorporated to the approaches as input through their innate natural language. Hence, in the second stage of this book, we worked on improving the outcomes of the approaches through the study of the natural language of the artifacts in use. To that extent, we studied: (1) the process of transforming the models into natural lan-guage and how it affects the approaches, published in (Lapeña, Pérez, and Cetina 2017), and (2) the impact of natural language processing over the approaches, published in (Lapeña, Font, Ó. Pastor, et al. 2017).

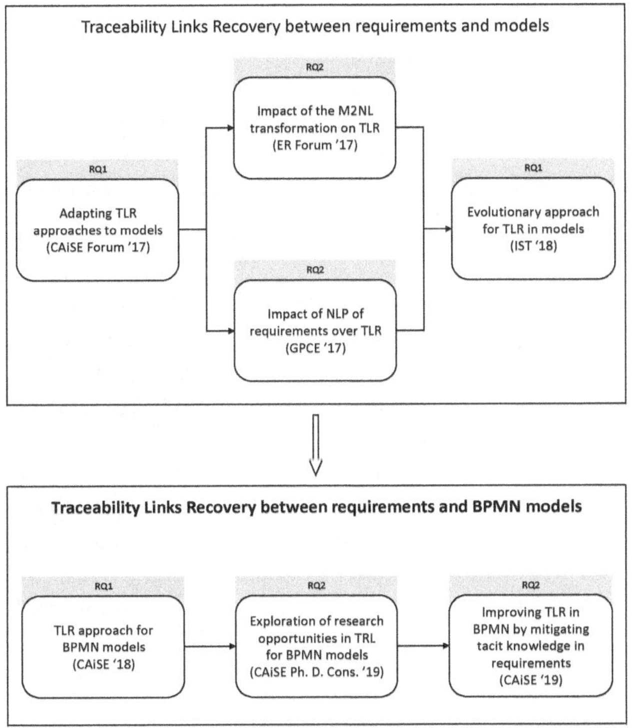

Figure 1: book work overview

The ideas and work up to this point, regarding Information Retrieval in model-based artifacts and Natural Language Processing of the artifacts in use, were extended and incorporated into a paper in the Information and Software Technology journal (Pérez et al. 2018) along with Feature Location and Bug Location ideas stemming from the research of other authors.

After the initial work on Traceability Links Recovery among natural language requirements and models, we started exploring the particularities of BPMN models. The first step in this novel stage of this thesis was to apply the enhanced approaches to BPMN models, comparing their results against state-of-the-art baselines.

The results of this work, which was published in (Lapeña, Font, Cetina, and O. Pastor 2018), brought to light certain particularities of the research challenge related to the requirements, the BPMN models, and their interaction within the context of the Traceability Links Recovery problem. We reviewed our latest research work and the arising challenges in the field t hrough a p aper i n t he C AiSE P hD C onsortium (Lapeña 2019).

In the final stage of this book, we have worked towards incorporating the particularities of the BPMN models case into the developed approaches for further improvement of the results. The first issue that we were able to identify was a misalignment between the language in the requirements and the BPMN models, in the form of tacit knowledge that was not made explicit in the requirements but that did appear in the BPMN models. We worked towards mitigating this language misalignment by expanding the requirements through the usage of a domain ontology, publishing the results in (Lapeña, Pérez, Cetina, and Ó. Pastor 2019). We also identified o ther p articularities w ithin t he l anguage i n u se i n t he BPMN models, which can also be leveraged to lead the approaches to enhanced results, and realized that BPMN models comprise less text than other kinds of software artifacts. These two last issues remain as future work.

book Structure

This book is conformed and presented as compendium of articles. According to the guidelines and regulations for the development of a PhD book in Universitat Politècnica de València, a PhD book that is presented as a compendium of articles must be structured in four parts:

I **Introduction:** The first part of the book (chapter 1) introduces the motivation for the research, the description of the problem along with the objectives of the work, the list of scientific articles published towards the fulfillment of the book goals, and the methodology that was followed to pursue the research presented in this book.

II Publications: The second part of the book (chapters 2 to 7) provides the compendium of scientific articles that result from the research that was carried out for the book. The contributions are ordered chronologically and adapted to the format of the book.

III Introduction: The third part of the book (chapter 8) discusses the results and contributions of the book to the research context, and the future works that arise as a continuation of the ongoing research.

IV Conclusions: The fourth and final part of the book (chapter 9) finishes the book by providing a few concluding remarks for the presented work.

The following section presents more information on the compendium of articles included in this book, and on their relationship with research questions, research projects, and case studies.

Articles Compendium

Figure 2 comprises a general overview of the research works that have been carried out as a result of this book. In the figure, it is possible to appreciate a total of five rows:

- The first row states the main objective of the book.

- The second row introduces the Research Questions posed by this book.

- The third row links the publications with the research questions posed by the book.

- The fourth row presents the research projects that served as a framework for the research.

- Finally, the fifth and final row indicates the industrial and academic case studies to which the book research has been applied.

book Objective	Analyze and improve Traceability Links Recovery between natural language requirements and BPMN models						
Research Questions	Adapt state-of-the-art approaches for TLR between requirements and BPMN models			Refine the approaches to improve the TLR process between requirements and BPMN models			
Publications	CAiSE Forum '17	IST '18	CAiSE '18	ER Forum '17	GPCE '17	CAiSE Ph. D. Consortium '19	CAiSE '19
Tools	FROM and LORE						
Research Projects	MINECO projects VARIAMOS (TIN2015-64397-R) and ALPS (RTI2018-096411-B-I00), ITEA REVaMP^2						
Case Studies	Construcción y Auxiliar de Ferrocarriles (CAF), software artifacts for industrial railway solutions Camunda BPMN for Research, academic case study						

Figure 2: book contributions overview

Several research articles have been developed as a result of the research that has been carried out for this **book**:

1. **Model Fragment Reuse Driven by Requirements (CAiSE Forum '17)** (Lapeña, Font, Cetina, and Ó. Pastor 2017): In this paper, we adapt the state of the art approaches in Information Retrieval in order to perform Traceability Links Recovery between natural language requirements and models.

2. **On the Influence of Models-to-Natural-Language Transformation in Traceability Link Recovery among Requirements and Conceptual Models (ER Forum '17)** (Lapeña, Pérez, and Cetina 2017): In our previous work, we realized that the necessary transformation of the models into natural language can affect the Traceability Links Recovery process. In this paper, we study the influence that the transformation from models into natural language has in the Traceability Links Recovery process, with the aim of improving the results obtained by the approaches.

3. **Analyzing the Impact of Natural Language Processing over Feature Location in Models (GPCE '17)** (Lapeña, Font, Ó. Pastor, et al. 2017): In the context of code-based software artifacts, processing the software artifacts in use through Natural Language Processing techniques is often considered beneficial for the outcomes of Information Retrieval processes. In this paper, we study the transportation and usage of the state-of-the-art Natural Language Processing techniques and their potential impact on Information Retrieval processes in the context of models.

4. **Fragment retrieval on models for model maintenance: Applying a multi-objective perspective to an industrial case study (IST '18)** (Pérez et al. 2018): This paper presents a novel approach that builds on prior work to retrieve the most relevant model fragments for different types of input queries, coming from three different Software Engineering tasks: Traceability Links Recovery, Bug Location, and Feature Location. We contributed to this research work by fully developing the studies on the Traceability Links Recovery part. The studies on Bug Location and Feature Location stem from the works of other authors in the same research environment.

5. **Exploring New Directions in Traceability Link Recovery in Models: the Process Models Case (CAiSE '18)** (Lapeña, Font, Cetina, and O. Pastor 2018): Through this paper, we apply the results of our prior research to adapt and propose novel and improved approaches for Traceability Links Recovery between requirements and models, putting the focus on BPMN models.

6. **Traceability Links Recovery in BPMN Models (Doctoral Consortium @ CAiSE '19)** (Lapeña 2019): In this paper, we recap the status of our work up to this point, highlighting our latest proposals and results, and explore ideas and opportunities for further improvements and future research within the context of the domain.

7. **Improving Traceability Links Recovery in Process Models through and Ontological Expansion of Requirements (CAiSE '19)** (Lapeña, Pérez, Cetina, and Ó. Pastor 2019): In prior works, we realized that the language in use in requirements is often incomplete, disregarding tacit knowledge (knowledge that is not specified in the requirements by the software engineers) that does appear in the models. This issue affects the Traceability Links Recovery process in a negative manner, since the language in the software artifacts ends up misaligned. Through this paper, we explore ways of aligning the language of the artifacts, through an ontological expansion of the requirements to palliate the amount and effect of tacit knowledge.

The works that conform this **book** have formed part of the research context of three funding projects: two Spanish national research plans named VARIAMOS (TIN2015-64397-R) and ALPS (RTI2018-096411-8-I00), devoted to the extraction of software variability in Software Product Lines, and one international project from the second call of European ITEA 3 projects named REVaMP^2, devoted to the creation of a holistic platform and process for variability extraction.

The approaches proposed as a result of this research have been validated through two case studies: (1) a proprietary industrial case study provided by one of our industrial partners, CAF (Construcciones y Auxiliar de Ferrocarriles), manufacturer of railway solutions, and (2) Camunda BPMN for Research, an academic case study freely available to the public. The various works presented in this **book** have led to the development of a series of frameworks and tools. Two of those tools, FROM and LORE, which are mentioned within the compendium of articles, are the culmination of the prototypes developed during the different stages of our research.

Research Methodology

For the development of this **book**, we have followed the methodology proposed by R. Wieringa (Wieringa 2014). Following the guidelines proposed in the methodology, we identified our research as design science research, since it is aimed at the resolution of a design problem. In that sense, our research emerges from the need to improve Traceability Links Recovery in the context of BPMN models, by developing novel Traceability Links Recovery approaches, such that they are applicable to the context with a measured degree of success, in order to help software engineers with the automation of this important, yet complex task.

The methodology is based on the iteration of design research cycles as the one depicted in Figure 3, consisting of the following phases:

1. **Problem investigation**: in this phase, we brought to light the main research problems, and formulated the appropriate research questions.

2. **Research design**: in this phase, we designed the approaches to respond to the research questions.

3. **Design validation**: in this phase, we studied the validity of the approaches through incorporating measurements commonly accepted by the research community and extensively used in the relevant literature. In addition, we studied the threats to the validity of the approaches and how to mitigate them.

4. **Research execution**: in this phase, we developed the approaches and applied them to the case studies to obtain results, which have been embodied into several research articles.

5. **Results evaluation**: in this phase, we analyzed the obtained results, obtaining responses to the posed research questions and identifying novel research opportunities in the process.

Figure 3: Research cycle

The cyclic process described in Figure 3 has been applied in an iterative fashion. Starting from the initial research challenge, the produced knowledge and the obtained results directed the initial research towards the arising perspectives. In this thesis, the first cycle started by transporting Traceability Links Recovery from code-based software artifacts towards model-based software artifacts. The responses to the research questions posed by the initial challenge triggered novel research questions, which acted as starting points for further research.

Part II

Compendium of Scientific Articles

Chapter 1

Model Fragment Reuse Driven by Requirements

Clone-and-Own is a common practice in families of software products, where parts from legacy products are reused in new developments. In industrial scenarios, CAO consumes high amounts of time and effort, not guaranteeing good results. We propose a novel approach, Computer Assisted CAO for Models (CACAO4M), that uses a Multi-Objective Evolutionary Algorithm (MOEA) with two objectives (Model Fragment Similitude, and Model Fragment Understandability) to rank relevant model fragments for reuse. We evaluated our approach in the industrial domain of train control software. Our approach outperforms the results of a baseline that uses only the Model Fragment Similitude metric, which encourages us to further research in this direction.

1.1 Introduction

Clone-And-Own (CAO) (Antkiewicz et al. 2014) is a common practice in the development of new products, consisting of adapting elements from legacy products in new product implementations. Reuse enables faster software development and easier tracking of projects, and helps maintain the development style and conventions consistent between products. In practice, CAO is carried out manually, relying on developers' knowledge of the family. In industrial scenarios, engineers tasked with new developments often lack knowledge over the entirety of the family, making CAO consume high amounts of time and effort, without guaranteeing good results.

This paper presents Computer Assisted Clone-And-Own for Models (CA-CAO4M), a novel approach for software families where products are developed through Model-Driven Development (MDD). The approach leverages the Multi-Objective Evolutionary Algorithm (MOEA) (Fonseca, Fleming, et al. 1993) technique to rank relevant model fragments for the requirements of a new development with two objectives: (1) the similitude of model fragments to the provided requirement, and (2) the understandability of model fragments from the perspective of a software engineer.

The results of our approach are evaluated in the domain of train control software with our industrial partner, CAF (`http://www.caf.net/en`), a worldwide provider of railway solutions, and compared against those of a baseline that takes in account only the similitude of model fragments to the provided requirement. The results of our approach improve those of the baseline, providing engineers with model fragments that are applicable to the problem requirement and easier to understand than those of the baseline, encouraging further research.

Through our work, Section 1.2 presents the background, Section 1.3 details our approach, Section 1.4 evaluates our approach, Section 1.5 gathers the related works, and Section 1.6 concludes the paper.

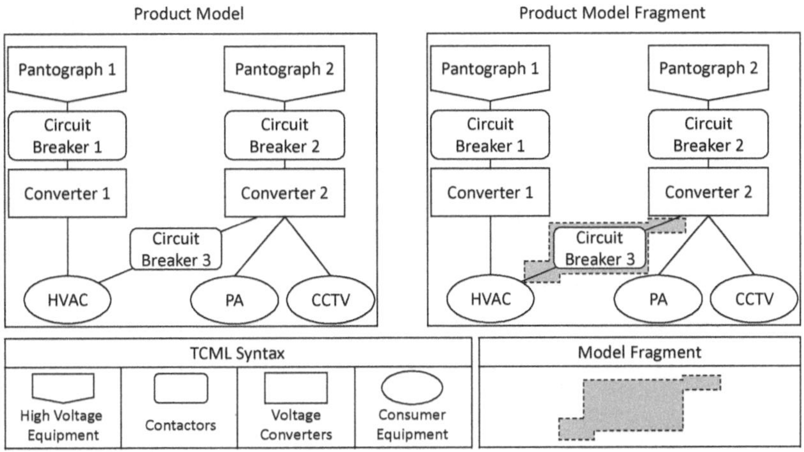

Figure 1.1: Example of TCML model and model fragment

1.2 Background

This section presents the Train Control and Management Language that formalizes the products from our industrial partner. It has the expressiveness required to (1) describe the interaction between train equipment, and (2) specify non-functional aspects. We present an equipment-focused simplified subset of TCML, along with a running example.

Fig. 1.1 depicts a real-world example model. The right part of Fig. 1.1 shows an example model fragment that realizes the "converter assistance" requirement, which allows the passing of current from one converter to equipment assigned to its peer to cover overload or failure. To formalize the model fragments used by CACAO4M, we use the Common Variability Language (CVL) (Haugen et al. 2008), which defines variants of a base model by replacing variable parts with alternative model replacements found in a library.

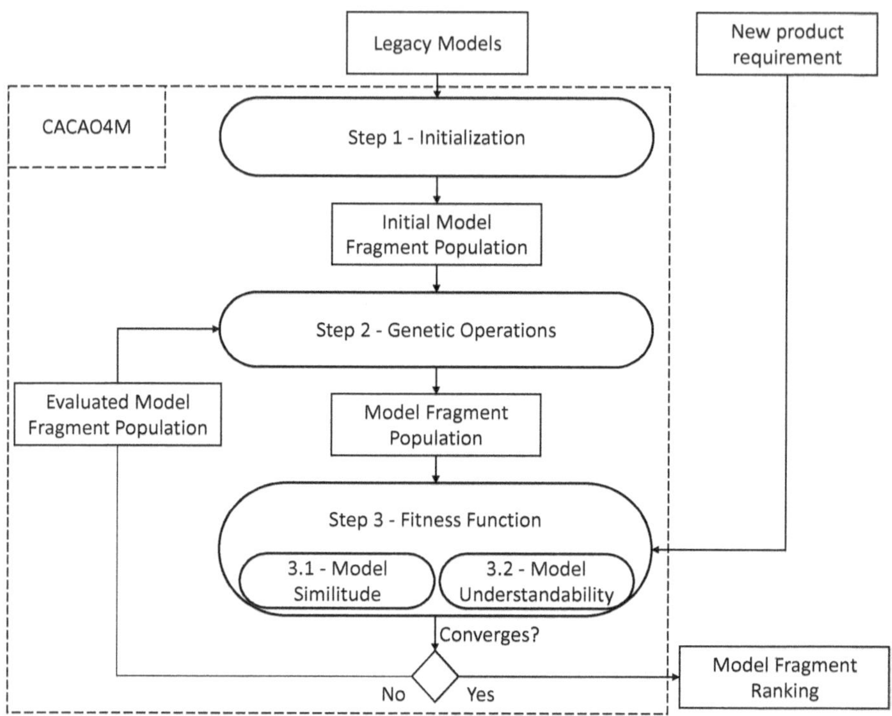

Figure 1.2: Approach Overview

1.3 Approach

Fig. 1.2 presents an overview of CACAO4M. As inputs, we use one requirement for a new product in the family, and the models that implement the legacy products in the family. Our approach runs in three steps: (1) **Initialization**, (2) application of **Genetic Operations**, and (3) **Fitness Function** assessing. The last two steps of the approach are repeated until the solution converges to a certain stop condition. When this occurs, the genetic algorithm provides a model fragment list, ranked according to the objectives, for the requirement.

1.3.1   Initialization & Genetic Operations

The first step of our approach generates an initial collection of model fragments, by randomly extracting parts of the legacy models.

The second step of our approach generates a set of model fragments that could realize the requirement. The generation of new model fragments is done by applying a set of three genetic operators, adapted to work over model fragments: selection of parents, crossover, and mutation. The **selection operator** picks the best candidates from the population as input for the rest of operators. We follow the wheel selection mechanism (Affenzeller et al. 2009), where each model fragment from the population has a probability of being selected proportional to its fitness score. The **crossover operation** enables the creation of a new individual by combining the genetic material from two parent model fragments. The **mutation operator** is used to imitate the mutations that randomly occur in nature when new individuals are born. The operations are taken from (Font et al. 2016a) and (Font et al. 2016b) respectively, where their application to models is detailed.

1.3.2   Model Fragment Fitness

The third step of the approach assesses each of the candidate model fragments, ranking them according to a fitness function. Our approach presents a fitness function based on two objectives: (1) the degree of similitude of the model fragment to the requirement, and (2) the understandability of the model fragment.

Model Fragment Similitude

To assess the relevance of each model fragment with relation to the provided requirement, we apply Latent Semantic Indexing (LSI) (Landauer, Foltz, and Laham 1998). LSI constructs vector representations of a query and a corpus of text documents by encoding them as a term-by-document co-occurrence matrix.

In our approach, terms are keywords extracted from requirements through natural language processing techniques, the documents are generated from the model fragments by extracting the terms that correspond to the elements that conform them, and the query is the provided requirement. Once the matrix is built, it is normalized and decomposed into a set of vectors using a matrix factorization technique called Singular Value Decomposition (SVD) (Landauer, Foltz, and Laham 1998). The similarity degree between the query and each document is calculated through the cosine between the vectors that represent them. Fig. 1.3 shows an example of co-occurrence matrix, taken from our approach. Fig. 1.3 also shows the result of applying the SVD technique to the matrix, and the scores associated to each model fragment.

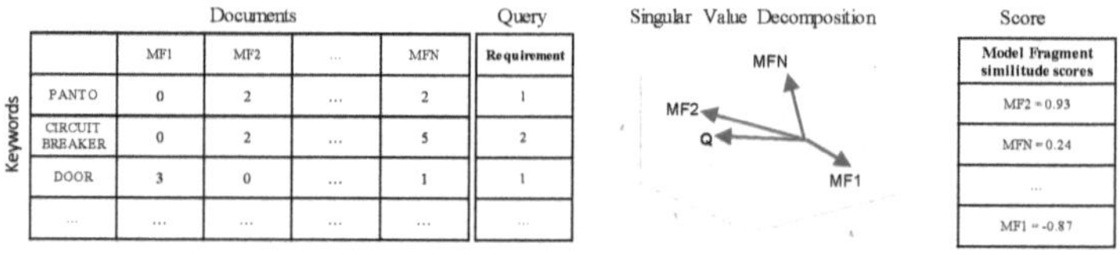

Figure 1.3: LSI example

Model Fragment Understandability

In order to measure the Understandability of a TCML model fragment, we measure its size by accounting the amount of lines, shapes, and labels that appear in the model fragment. As an example, we highlight the calculations for the model on Fig. 1.1. To compute the Understandability metric, we take in account the number of lines (9) and the number of shapes (10), for a total of 19 model elements.

1.4   Evaluation

This section evaluates our approach by applying it to a case study from our industrial partner consisting of 23 trains, each one having an associated requirements specification document, and an associated model.

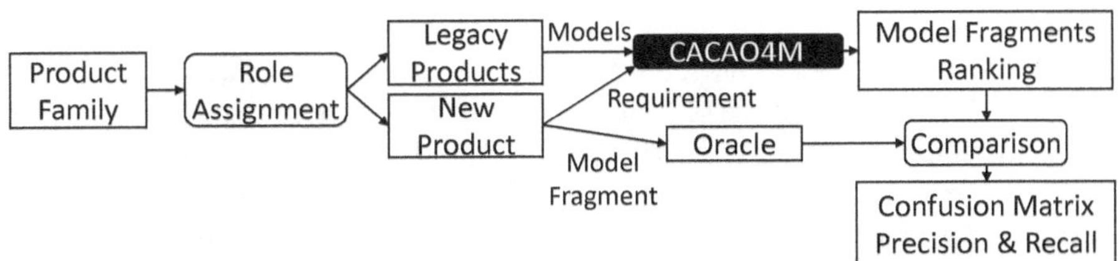

Figure 1.4: Evaluation Steps

Requirements from the document are implemented through model fragments in the model. The documents specify, on average, around 420 requirements each. The models comprise, on average, around 1200 elements each.

1.4.1 Experimental Setup

Fig. 1.4 shows the steps followed to evaluate our approach. First, roles are assigned to products in the product family. One product acts as the new product and the rest act as legacy products. The models of the products that act as legacy products, and one requirement of the product that acts as the new product are used to perform CACAO4M, while the model fragment that implements the latter is kept apart to be used as an oracle. Therefore, in order for a product to act as an oracle, it is necessary to have the mapping between its requirements and the model fragments that implement each of them. From the 23 products in the family, the mapping is available for 4. These products are the ones that can be used as oracles in our family.

Then, CACAO4M performs the steps described in our approach to provide a model fragment ranking for the requirement of the new product. We carry out the genetic algorithm inside CACAO4M, weighing the two metrics (Model Similitude and Model Understandability) as 90% - 10%. We also apply CACAO4M with a 100% - 0% weighing, to simulate a Single Objective Evolutionary Algorithm (SOEA) where only Model Similitude is taken in account. The SOEA is considered as the baseline against which the results of the MOEA are compared.

Finally, the first model fragment in the ranking for each result is compared with the oracle model fragment, in order to obtain a confusion matrix. A confusion matrix is a table used to describe the performance of a classification model (in this case, our algorithms) on a set of test data (the resulting model fragments) for which the true values are known (from the oracle). Each solution outputted by the algorithm is a model fragment composed of a subset of the model elements that are part of the product model (where the requirement is being located). Since the granularity is at the level of model elements, each model element presence or absence is considered as a classification.

The confusion matrix distinguishes between the predicted values and the real values classifying them into four categories: (1) **True Positive (TP):** predicted true - real true; (2) **False Positive (FP):** predicted true - real false; (3) **True Negative (TN):** predicted false - real false; and (4) **False Negative (FN):** predicted false - real true. The evaluated performance metrics are:

(1) **Precision**: number of elements from the solution that are correct according to the ground truth, expressed as

$$Precision = \frac{TP}{TP + FP} \tag{1.1}$$

(2) **Recall**: number of elements of the solution retrieved by the proposed solution, expressed as

$$Recall = \frac{TP}{TP + FN} \tag{1.2}$$

(3) **F-measure**: harmonic mean of precision and recall, expressed as

$$F - measure = \frac{2 * TP}{2 * TP + FP + FN} \tag{1.3}$$

We perform our evaluation separately for every requirement in an oracle, and for all the 4 possible oracles individually.

1.4.2 Results

The LSI 90% & U 10% (MOEA) achieves the best results, providing a mean precision value of 55.34%, a recall value of 49.98%, and a combined F-measure of 52.52%; while the LSI 100% & U 0% (SOEA) achieves a mean precision value of 53.21%, a recall value of 49.73%, and a combined F-measure of 51.41%.

1.5 Related Work

Feature location approaches in a product family such as the one presented in (Xue, Xing, and Jarzabek 2012) center their efforts in finding the code that implements a feature between the different products by combining techniques such as FCA and LSI. We are not interested in the code representation of a feature in the family, but in locating the most relevant model fragments that implement a requirement.

Works as (Wille et al. 2013) focus on the location of features over models by comparing the models with each other to formalize the variability among them in the form of a Software Product Line. We do not locate features, but model fragments that implement requirements, and our goal is not to formalize variability, but to help engineers develop requirements through model fragment Clone-And-Own.

Font et al. (Font et al. 2016a) use a SOEA to locate features among a family of models in the form of a variation point. Their approach is refined in (Font et al. 2016b), where a SOEA is used to find sets of suitable feature realizations. The presented approach, in contrast, locates model fragments that are relevant for the development of a single requirement. The presented approach also differs from (Font et al. 2016a) and (Font et al. 2016b) both technique and metrics, by using a MOEA, with a fitness function that combines Model Similitude and Model Understandability.

In (Lapeña, Ballarín, and Cetina 2016), Lapeña et. al use POS Tagging in combination with an adapted two-step LSI to obtain rankings of methods for all the requirements of a new product in a product family.

In the presented work, we obtain only one ranking for one requirement on demand. Plus, this approach uses a MOEA, against the modified LSI in (Lapeña, Ballarín, and Cetina 2016). Finally, the scope of this work is centered around finding models that can be used to implement a particular requirement, not finding relevant code for requirements implementation.

1.6 Conclusions

Clone-And-Own (CAO) is a common practice in the development of new products in families of software products. In practice, it is carried out manually and relies on human factors, consuming high amounts of time and effort without guaranteeing good results. This paper presents Computer Assisted Clone-And-Own for Models (CACAO4M), a novel approach that leverages a MOEA to rank relevant model fragments for the development of particular requirements for a new product. CACAO4M assesses the similitude of model fragments to the provided requirement, and their understandability. Through our approach, we aim to prioritize the model fragments that are easier to understand from the perspective of a software engineer. Our MOEA approach is evaluated against a SOEA baseline that takes in account only model fragment similitude, outperforming the baseline in every performance indicator. Model Understandability provides a way of locating model fragments that are applicable to the problem requirement and easier to understand than those retrieved by the SOEA. Results encourage us to work further in this direction.

Chapter 2

On the Influence of M2NL Transformation in TLR among Requirements and Conceptual Models

Recovering traceability links between software artifacts and requirements is a common task in Software Engineering. Information Retrieval (IR) techniques have been applied to recover traceability links amongst code and requirements. By transforming Models into Natural Language (M2NL), it is possible to apply IR to calculate their traceability links to requirements. However, results retrieved by IR are affected by the writing style of the NL input. Regarding M2NL, there are two main types of techniques in use: Rule-Based techniques, and Element-Based techniques. Along with M2NL, there is a wide range of Natural Language Processing (NLP) techniques that can be applied. Through this work, we analyze how the usage of distinct M2NL-NLP combinations of techniques impacts IR-based Traceability Links Recovery over requirements and models. We evaluate two different M2NL techniques, and the inclusion of Simple and Advanced NLP along with M2NL, in a real-world industrial case study.

2.1   Introduction

Traceability Links Recovery (TLR) between software artifacts and requirements is a common task in Software Engineering (SE), specially when maintaining and evolving software products. For code and Natural Language (NL) requirements, Information Retrieval (IR) techniques have been successfully used for TLR. By transforming conceptual models into NL, it is possible to apply IR to requirements-models TLR. However, results retrieved by these techniques depend greatly in the style in which NL is written. Two main types of techniques are applied for Models-to-Natural-Language Transformation (M2NL): Rule-Based techniques (Meziane, Athanasakis, and Ananiadou n.d.), and Element-Based techniques (Font et al. 2016). Rule-Based techniques apply sets of logical and grammatical rules, while Element-Based techniques extract text associated to model elements directly.

After the M2NL transformation process, there is a wide range of Natural Language Processing (NLP) techniques that are applied to process NL representations of models. Some of them are: general phrase styling techniques, syntactical analysis techniques (Hulth n.d.), semantic analysis techniques (Plisson, Lavrac, Mladenic, et al. n.d.), and human-in-the-loop techniques. These techniques are combined in distinct ways by different authors, depending on implementation circumstances and research particularities.

The impact of the usage of different M2NL-NLP techniques combinations on requirements-models TLR has not been studied yet. Through this work, we analyze how distinct M2NL-NLP techniques combinations impact requirements-models TLR through Latent Semantic Indexing (LSI) (Landauer, Foltz, and Laham 1998), the technique that obtains the best TLR results (Poshyvanyk et al. 2007). We evaluate two different M2NL techniques and the inclusion of Simple and Advanced NLP along with M2NL, in a real-world industrial case study in the rolling stocks domain with our industrial partner, CAF[1] (Construcciones y Auxiliar de Ferrocarriles).

The combination of Rule-Based M2NL with Advanced NLP leads LSI to the best results, returning the model fragments that materialize requirements in an average ranking position of 1 ± 1.12. However, in order to use Rule-Based M2NL, engineers must adapt or create rules for their Domain Specific Language (DSL). The combination of Element-Based M2NL with Advanced NLP returns a worse result for the same measurement (2 ± 5.09), but does not require said efforts.

The paper is structured as follows: Section 2.2 presents our Approach. Section 2.3 details the Evaluation designed to tackle the Research Questions. Section 2.4 analyzes the statistical significance of the obtained results. Section 2.5 presents the Threats to Validity of our work. Section 2.6 summarizes the works related to the presented paper. Finally, Section 2.7 concludes the paper.

2.2 Approach

So far, there has been no discussion on which Model-to-Natural-Language Transformation (M2NL) techniques should be applied for requirements-models Traceability Links Recovery (TLR). The effect of the inclusion of Simple or Advanced Natural Language Processing (NLP) techniques along with M2NL to the same intent has not been studied yet either. The presented approach studies the impact of using two different M2NL techniques, and the impact of including Simple or Advanced NLP techniques along M2NL, over a widely accepted TLR technique, Latent Semantic Indexing (LSI). Analyzing the success of LSI over the different inputs, we aim to determine which one guides LSI to enhanced results.

The top part of Fig. 2.1 depicts the outline of this work. Through the usage of M2NL techniques, we convert model fragments into NL. Then, we process the NL representation of the models and a NL requirement from our case study through NLP techniques. With the processed model fragments and requirement, we carry out LSI, ranking the model fragments according to their similitude to the query requirement. The bottom part of Fig. 2.1 shows the four configurations considered through this work, which we analyze in order to determine their impact on requirements-models TLR.

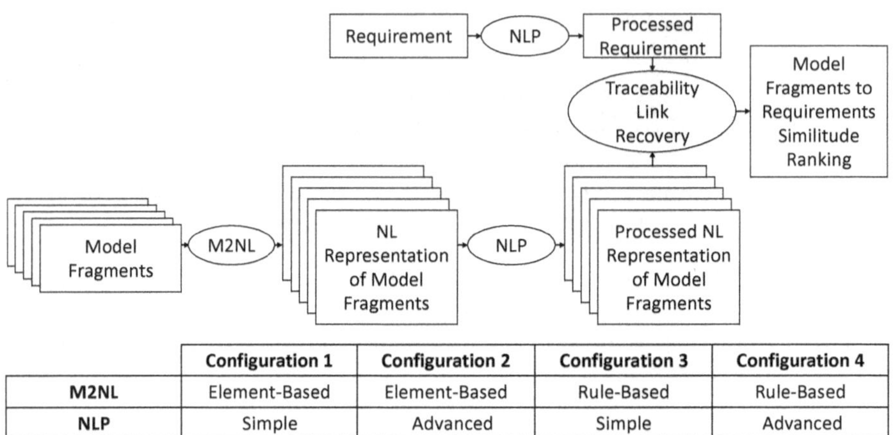

	Configuration 1	Configuration 2	Configuration 3	Configuration 4
M2NL	Element-Based	Element-Based	Rule-Based	Rule-Based
NLP	Simple	Advanced	Simple	Advanced

Figure 2.1: Traceability Link Recovery among Requirements and Conceptual Models Overview

The following subsections describe the M2NL techniques taken in account through the rest of this work, the NLP techniques used to process the NL representations of the model fragments and requirements in the case study, and the LSI technique from which results are extracted.

2.2.1 *Models-to-Natural-Language Transformation Techniques (M2NL)*

In order to extract NL from models, two main techniques are applied in the literature: Rule-Based, and Element-Based M2NL. Fig. 2.2 depicts an example DSL model from our industrial partner (where the company-specific DSL in use is TCML, Train Control Modeling Language), and shows the results of applying both Rule-Based and Element-Based M2NL to the model. In order to formalize model fragments, we use the Common Variability Language (CVL) (Haugen et al. 2008).

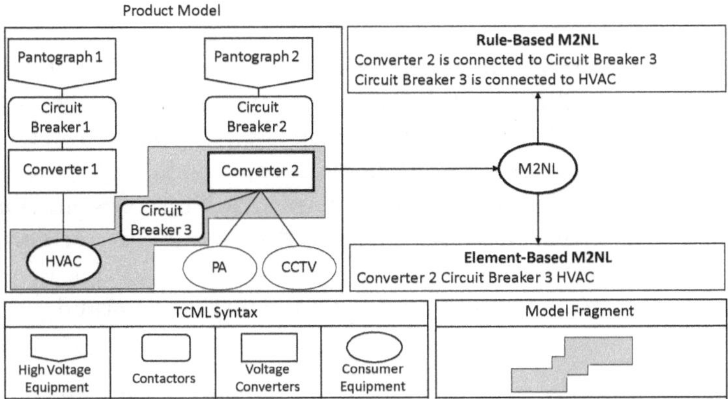

Figure 2.2: Example of TCML model and model fragment

Rule-Based M2NL

This technique uses a set of user-defined rules to process text inside models. Through the rules, several aspects inherent to modeling language (such as naming conventions, model element types, grammatical element ordering, etc.) are exploited to generate semantically sound NL representations of models.

We use the Rule-Based M2NL technique presented by Meziane et. al. in (Meziane, Athanasakis, and Ananiadou n.d.), where the authors research the language used in class diagrams components and develop rules for semantically sound NL generation. The TCML used by our industrial partner was developed following UML conventions, with equipment elements corresponding to UML classes, equipment properties corresponding to UML attributes, and connections corresponding to UML relationships. We can leverage the rules in (Meziane, Athanasakis, and Ananiadou n.d.) to generate NL representations of the TCML models. As an example, for the model fragment depicted in the top left part of Fig. 2.2, this technique would yield the following strings: 'Converter 2 is connected to Circuit Breaker 3', and 'Circuit Breaker 3 is connected to HVAC'.

Element-Based M2NL

This technique is used in approaches that concur M2NL for Feature Location (Font et al. 2016) and Software Product Lines synthesis (Zhang, Haugen, and Moller-Pedersen 2011) purposes. Through this technique, the NL texts that represent each element of a model are extracted and then concatenated into a single string, used as a NL representation of the model. The NL representations generated through this technique vary in understandability, being commonly closer to a collection of words or expressions than to descriptions of functionality understandable by humans.

For the TCML models from our industrial partner, we use this technique by extracting the text from all the model elements. As an example, for the model fragment depicted in the top left part of Fig. 2.2, this technique would yield the string 'Converter 2 Circuit Breaker HVAC'. Fig. 2 is, for understandability purposes and space reasons, a simplification of a real model. In a real model, model elements contain more properties which in turn yield more text in its NL representation.

2.2.2 NLP Techniques

Fig. 2.3 depicts the NLP techniques used through this work, along with an example taken from a real-world train. In Fig. 2.3, a NL requirement is used as the input for the example, but through our work, these techniques are applied to both NL requirements and NL representations of models obtained through the application of either Rule-Based M2NL or Element-Based M2NL (see top part of Fig. 2.1).

Through this work, we include either Simple or Advanced NLP along with M2NL. Simple NLP uses the techniques in 2.2.2, since we consider their combination to be the most basic unit of NLP. Advanced NLP includes the techniques that conform Simple NLP, plus those described in 2.2.2, 2.2.2, and 2.2.2.

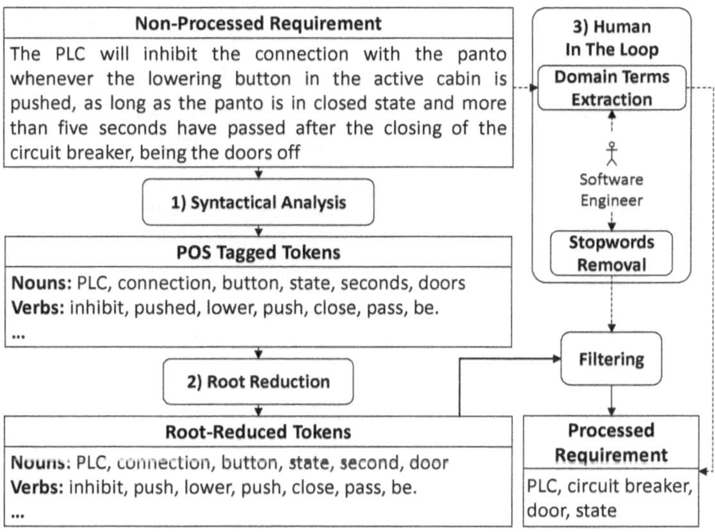

Figure 2.3: Compendium of NLP Techniques

Syntactical Analysis

Syntactical Analysis (SA) techniques determine the grammatical function of words in sentences (e.g.: nouns, verbs, etc.). These techniques, often referred to as Parts-Of-Speech (POS) Tagging, allow engineers to implement grammatical filters, usually in search for nouns, which often carry relevant information on features and actions (Capobianco et al. n.d.). Words like verbs or adjectives are often disregarded. In Fig. 2.3, it is possible to appreciate the SA process, with the POS Tagged Tokens as outcome of syntactically analyzing a real-world NL requirement. Nouns and verbs are depicted while, for space reasons, the rest of the words are omitted.

Root Reduction

Through the usage of semantic techniques such as Lemmatizing, words can be reduced to their semantic roots (lemmas). Through lemmas, it is possible to unify NL, avoiding verb tenses, plurals, and strange word forms that interfere with TLR. Prior to carrying out Root Reduction (RR) techniques, it is imperative to use SA techniques, since RR techniques are based on word dictionaries built upon the grammatical role of words. Semantic techniques provide more advanced word filters in NL requirements. In Fig. 2.3, it is possible to appreciate the RR process, with the Root-Reduced Tokens as outcome of the semantic analysis of the POS Tags derived from the NL requirement. The lemmas of nouns and verbs are depicted while, for space reasons, the rest of the words are omitted.

Human-In-The-Loop

The inclusion of domain experts in TLR processes is a widely discussed topic within SE. It is often beneficial to have domain knowledge embedded in TLR, particularly for software reuse and variability. Some of the human interaction techniques used in TLR are Domain Terms Extraction and Stopwords Removal. In order to carry out these techniques, engineers provide two separate lists of terms: one list of both single-word and multiple-word terms that belong to the domain and must be kept for analysis, and a list of irrelevant words that have no analysis value. Both kinds of terms can be automatically filtered in or out of the final query. In Fig. 2.3, it is possible to appreciate the Human-In-The-Loop process, where a software engineer provides both lists of terms, which are consequently introduced into the final query, or filtered out of it.

Other Filters

The most basic NLP technique covered in this work is the combination of tokenizing and lowercasing a sentence, and afterwards removing duplicate words from it. This combination is often regarded as the most basic NLP technique for several LSI examples.

2.2.3 Traceability Link Recovery through Latent Semantic Indexing

Latent Semantic Indexing (LSI) is an automatic mathematical/statistical technique that analyzes relationships between *queries* and *documents* (bodies of text). It constructs vector representations of both a user *query* and a corpus of text *documents* by encoding them as a *term-by-document co-occurrence matrix*, and analyzes the relationships between those vectors to get a similarity ranking between the *query* and the *documents*. Fig. 2.4 shows an example *term-by-document co-occurrence matrix*, with values associated to our case study, the vectors, and the resulting ranking. In the following paragraphs, an overview of the elements of the matrix is provided.

Terms: Each row in the matrix (*term*) stands for each of the words that compose the processed requirement and NL representations of model fragments. In Fig. 2.4, it is possible to appreciate a set of representative words in the domain such as 'pantograph' or 'doors' as the *terms* of each row.

Documents: Each column in the matrix stands for the processed NL representation of each model fragment in our case study. In Fig. 2.4, it is possible to appreciate the identifiers of the model fragments in the columns such as 'M_KAO001' or 'M_CIN072', which stand for the processed NL representations of those particular model fragments.

Query: The final column stands for the *query*. In our approach, the *query* is one processed requirement in our case study. In Fig. 2.4, the identifier of the requirement in the *query* column ('R_BUD010') represents its processed text.

Data: Each cell in the matrix contains the frequency with which the *term* of its row appears in the *document* denoted by its column. For instance, in Fig. 2.4, the *term* 'pantograph' appears twice in the 'M_KAO001' processed NL representation and once in the 'R_BUD010' processed requirement.

We obtain vector representations of the *documents* and the *query* by normalizing and decomposing the *term-by-document co-occurrence matrix* using a matrix factorization technique called *Singular Value Decomposition* (SVD) (Landauer, Foltz, and Laham 1998). SVD is a form of factor analysis, or more properly the mathematical generalization of which factor analysis is a special case. In SVD, a rectangular matrix is decomposed into the product of three other matrices. One component matrix describes the original row entities as vectors of derived orthogonal factor values, another describes the original column entities in the same way, and the third is a diagonal matrix containing scaling values such that when the three components are matrix-multiplied, the original matrix is reconstructed.

In Fig. 2.4, a three-dimensional graph of the SVD is provided. On the graph, it is possible to appreciate the vectorial representations of some of the matrix columns. For space reasons, only a small set of the columns is represented. To measure the similarity degree between vectors, our approach calculates the cosine between the *query* vector and the *documents* vectors. Cosine values closer to one denote a higher degree of similarity, and cosine values closer to minus one denote a lower degree of similarity. Similarity increases as vectors point in the same general direction (as more *terms* are shared between *documents*). Through this measurement, our approach orders the model fragments according to their similarity degree to the requirement.

The relevancy ranking (which can be seen in Fig. 2.4) is produced according to the calculated similarity degrees. In this example, LSI retrieves 'M_BUD010' and 'M_KAO001' in the first and second position of the relevancy ranking due to *query-documents* cosines being '0.9243' and '0.8454', implying a high similarity degree between the fragments and the requirement. On the opposite, the 'M_CIN072' is returned in a latter position of the ranking due to its *query-document* cosine being '-0.7836', implying a lower similarity degree.

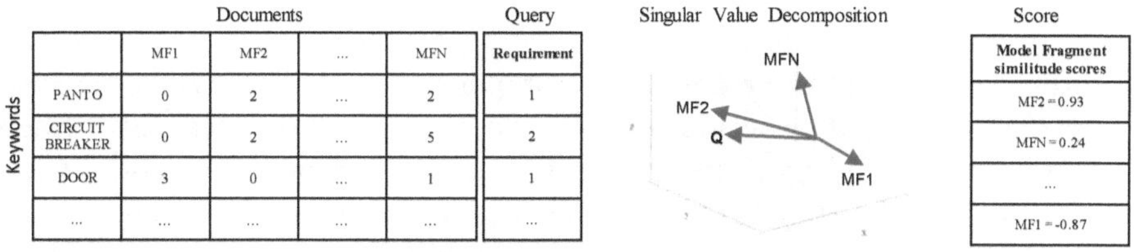

	Documents				Query
	MF1	MF2	...	MFN	Requirement
PANTO	0	2	...	2	1
CIRCUIT BREAKER	0	2	...	5	2
DOOR	3	0	...	1	1
...	...	...	...	...	...

Singular Value Decomposition

Score

Model Fragment similitude scores
MF2 = 0.93
MFN ≈ 0.24
...
MF1 = -0.87

Figure 2.4: Traceability Link Recovery through Latent Semantic Indexing Example

2.3 Evaluation

Through the following paragraphs, we present the research questions that our work tackles, describe our real-world case study and the oracle used for our experiment, detail the design of our experiment, and present the obtained results.

2.3.1 Research Questions

From the described problem, two research questions arise:

RQ1: How does the usage of different M2NL techniques affect the effectiveness and efficiency of TLR over requirements and models?

RQ2: How does the inclusion of either Simple or Advanced NLP techniques along with M2NL affect the effectiveness and efficiency of TLR over requirements and models?

2.3.2 Case study

For our experiment, CAF provided us with requirements and models of five railway solutions from Auckland, Bucharest, Cincinnati, Houston, and Kaohsiung. The trains are specified by about 100 requirements each, with an average of 50 words. Regarding models, trains are specified through an average 8250 model elements. CAF also provided lists of domain terms and stopwords. The domain terms list comprehends around 300 domain terms, and the stopwords list comprehends around 60 words. Both lists were created by a CAF domain expert associated to the provided products.

2.3.3 Oracle

In order to evaluate the results of our experiment, CAF provided us with their existing documentation on requirements-models traceability. Each requirement can be mapped to a single model fragment. A model fragment is a model elements subset, specified with the model fragment formalization capacities of the Common Variability Language (CVL) (Haugen et al. 2008). We use the existing traceability as the oracle for evaluating the impact of each of the M2LN-NLP configurations on LSI. To achieve this, we analyze the results of the rankings generated by LSI, checking the position of the ranking in which the oracle (correct model fragment for the input requirement) appears.

2.3.4 Design of the experiment

The first step is to select a M2NL-NLP configuration. With the chosen configuration, we extract the NL representation of the model fragments in our case study. Then, we perform the necessary NLP over the text of both all the requirements and all the NL representations of model fragments in our case study.

From the strings achieved through the first step, all the individual words are extracted to form a list of words. The list of words (*terms*), the processed representations of model fragments (*documents*), and one processed requirement (*query*), are used as input for LSI. LSI returns a ranking of model fragments, ordered according to their similarity to the requirement. LSI is performed several times, taking each requirement from our case study as *query*, in order to extract the model fragment rankings for all the available requirements. Through these rankings and the oracle, we can determine the ranking positions in which the correct model fragments appear for each requirement. Through the results, we are able to evaluate the impact of the chosen M2NL-NLP configuration over LSI.

The described steps (choosing a configuration, performing NLP of requirements and model fragments, LSI, impact analysis) are carried out four times, until the four configurations are chosen and analyzed.

2.3.5 Results

For each M2NL-NLP configuration, we measured the average, best, and worst result in the rankings generated by LSI. We also measured the time that the execution of M2NL-NLP took for the different configurations on average after 25 executions. We do not highlight the LSI execution time averages, since it is practically identical for all the configurations (around 70 seconds). Table 2.1 shows the results achieved by LSI when performed over the four configurations, with the best results highlighted in light gray.

Table 2.1: Results per M2NL-NLP techniques configuration

	Average Result ± Standard Deviation	Best Result	Worst Result	Time Taken (s)
Configuration 1	#2 ± 5.54	#1	#34	12
Configuration 2	#2 ± 5.09	#1	#30	296
Configuration 3	#1 ± 2.75	#1	#19	53
Configuration 4	#1 ± 1.12	#1	#5	336

Configuration 4 (Rule-Based M2NL + Advanced NLP) leads LSI to the best results, retrieving an average ranking position of #1 ± 1.12, a ranking position #1 as its best result, and a ranking position #5 as its worst. Configuration 1 (Element-Based M2NL + Simple NLP), on the opposite, is the one that leads LSI to the worst results. Its best result is position #1, but its worst peaks at position #34, presenting an average of #2 ± 5.54. Configurations 2 (Element-Based M2NL + Advanced NLP) and 3 (Rule-Based M2NL + Simple NLP) present intermediate values, being Configuration 3 slightly better than Configuration 2.

2.4 Statistical analysis

To properly compare the different configurations, the data resulting from the empirical analysis was analyzed using statistical methods.

2.4.1 Statistical significance

A statistical test must be run to assess whether there is enough empirical evidence to claim that there is a difference between two configurations (e.g., A is better than B). To achieve this, two hypotheses are defined: the null hypothesis H_0, and the alternative hypothesis H_1. The null hypothesis H_0 is typically defined to state that there is no difference among the configurations, whereas the alternative hypothesis H_1 states that the configurations differ. In such a case, a statistical test aims to verify whether the null hypothesis H_0 should be rejected.

The statistical tests provide a probability value, $p-value$. The $p-value$ obtains values between 0 and 1. The lower the $p-value$ of a test, the more likely that the null hypothesis is false. It is accepted by the research community that a $p-value$ under 0.05 is statistically significant (Arcuri and Briand 2014), and so the hypothesis H_0 can be considered false. The carried test depends on the properties of the data. Since our data does not follow a normal distribution in general, our analysis requires the use of non-parametric techniques. There are several tests for analyzing this kind of data; however, the Quade test is the most powerful when working with real data (García et al. 2010). In addition, according to Conover (Conover 1999), the Quade test is the one that has shown the best results for a low number of configurations.

The $p-Value$ of this test is $4.208x10^{-6}$ and the statistic of this test is 9.659. Since the $p-Value$ is smaller than 0.05, we reject the null hypothesis. Consequently, we can state that there exist differences between among the four configurations for the performance indicator of the position in the ranking.

However, with the Quade test, we cannot answer the following question: *Which of the configurations gives the best performance?* In this case, the performance of each configuration should be individually compared against all other alternatives. In order to do this, we perform an additional post hoc analysis. This kind of analysis performs a pairwise comparison among the results of each configuration, determining whether statistically significant differences exist among the results of a specific pair of configurations.

The second column of Table 2.2 shows the $p - Values$ of Holm's post hoc analysis for the performance indicator and the specific pair of configurations (e.g., Configuration 1 and Configuration 2). The $p - Values$ shown in this table for two comparisons (the Configuration 1 vs Configuration 2 and Configuration 3 vs Configuration 4) are greater than the corresponding significance threshold value (0.05), whereas the $p-Values$ for the other comparisons are smaller than 0.05. Hence, we can determine that the differences in performance between the Configuration 1 vs Configuration 2 and the Configuration 3 vs Configuration 4 are not significant, but the differences in performance are significant in the other comparisons (e.g., the comparison shows significant differences between the Configuration 2 vs Configuration 4).

2.4.2   Effect size

Statistically significant differences can be obtained even if they are so small as to be of no practical value (Arcuri and Briand 2014). Therefore, it is important to assess if a configuration is statistically better than another and to assess the magnitude of the improvement. *Effect size* measures are taken in account to analyze this phenomenon. For a non-parametric effect size measure, we use Vargha and Delaney's $\hat{A}_{12}$ (Vargha and Delaney 2000). $\hat{A}_{12}$ measures the probability that running one configuration yields higher values than running another configuration. If the two configurations are equivalent, then $\hat{A}_{12}$ will be 0.5.

For example, $\hat{A}_{12} = 0.7$ means that we would obtain better results in 70% of the runs with the first of the pair of configurations that have been compared, and $\hat{A}_{12} = 0.3$ means that we would obtain better results in 70% of the runs with the second of the pair of configurations that have been compared. Thus, we have an $\hat{A}_{12}$ value for every pair of configurations.

The third column of Table 2.2 shows the values of the effect size statistics between every pair of configurations. The $\hat{A}_{12}$ values show a slight superiority (even though these values are closer to the equivalent value of 0.5) of the Configuration 2 in the comparison with the Configuration 1, and the Configuration 3 in the comparison with the Configuration 4.

The $\hat{A}_{12}$ values show the largest differences, with values around 0.39 when Configuration 1 and Configuration 2 are compared with Configuration 3 or Configuration 4. Overall, these results confirm that Configuration 3 and Configuration 4 outperform Configuration 1 and Configuration 2.

Table 2.2: Holm's post hoc $p - Values$ and $\hat{A}_{12}$ statistic for each pair of configurations

Pair of configurations	$p - Value$	$\hat{A}_{12}$
Configuration 1 vs Configuration 2	0.89	0.4983
Configuration 1 vs Configuration 3	0.0065	0.3948
Configuration 1 vs Configuration 4	0.00079	0.4005
Configuration 2 vs Configuration 3	0.0024	0.3883
Configuration 2 vs Configuration 4	$3.4x10^{-5}$	0.3973
Configuration 3 vs Configuration 4	0.83	0.5122

2.5 Threats to Validity

In this section, we use the classification of threats of validity of (Wohlin et al. 2012) to acknowledge the limitations of our approach:

1 **Construct Validity:** This aspect of validity reflects the extent to which the operational measures that are studied represent what the researchers have in mind. In order to minimize this risk, we study the positions of the oracles in the rankings, an objective and widely accepted measure, used before by other researchers in the community (Haiduc et al. 2013).

2 **Internal Validity:** This aspect of validity is of concern when causal relations are examined. There is a risk that the factor being investigated may be affected by other neglected factors. The number of requirements and models presented in this work may look small, but they implement a wide scope of different railway equipment.

3 **External Validity:** This aspect of validity is concerned with to what extent it is possible to generalize the finding, and to what extent the findings are of relevance for other cases. Both requirements and conceptual models are frequently leveraged to specify all kinds of different software. LSI is a widely accepted and utilized technique which has proven to obtain good results in multiple domains.

Therefore, our experiment does not rely on the particular conditions of our domain. Nonetheless, the experiment and its results should be replicated in other domains before assuring their generalization.

4 Reliability: This aspect is concerned with to what extent the data and the analysis are dependent on the specific researchers. The requirements and models of the trains used through our experiment were provided by our industrial partner engineers, as well as the domain terms and stopwords lists, which were crafted by domain experts not involved in this research.

2.6   Related Work

In (Falessi, Cantonc, and Canfora 2013), NLP techniques are used to assess equivalence between requirements. The authors conclude that performance of NLP in their field is determined by the properties of the provided datasets. Properties are then considered as a factor to adjust the NLP process and performance over an industrial case study. Through our work, rather than adjusting the NLP process to study equivalence between requirements, we tackle the impact of different M2NL-NLP configurations on LSI, exposing the way they behave and improve (or worsen) the IR process.

The work presented in (Arora et al. 2015) uses NLP to study how changes in requirements impact other requirements. The authors analyze TLR between requirements, and use NLP to determine the propagation of changes. Our work does not analyze changes in requirements or how they affect the system, but rather on what is the most appropriate way of applying M2NL-NLP to requirements-models TLR. Moreover, the authors of (Arora et al. 2015) do not consider different NLP configurations, but rather guide the process through requirements properties.

Finally, (Eder et al. 2015) takes in consideration the possible LSI configurations for TLR between requirements and test cases. The authors state that LSI configurations depend on the available datasets, and also look forward to automatically determining appropriate LSI configurations for any given dataset.

We do not tackle the impact of using different LSI configurations for TLR, but rather analyze how different M2NL-NLP configurations affect the results of TLR.

2.7 Conclusions

Through this paper, we analyze how different M2NL-NLP techniques impact the outcome of requirements-models TLR. To that extent, we process the requirements and models that specify a real-world industrial case study through a series of combinations of M2NL-NLP techniques, and then perform Latent Semantic Indexing (LSI) over the processed specifications. We study the rankings produced by LSI with our oracle to evaluate the impact of the M2NL-NLP techniques over TLR. Results show that:

1 Rule-Based M2NL improves the results of Element-Based M2NL in a statistically significant manner, but it requires an additional effort from software engineers when Domain Specific Languages (DSLs) are used. The rules from (Meziane, Athanasakis, and Ananiadou n.d.) are specific for UML models, and work with the TCML DSL of our industrial partner due to it being derived from UML, but engineers that use a non-UML DSL need to either adapt the existing rules or create DSL-specific rules. With the obtained results, engineers have more information to choose between investing their efforts in Rule-Based M2NL, or (in case it yields sufficiently reliable TLR results) using Element-Based M2NL.

2 The usage of Advanced NLP along with M2NL always improves its results, although in a non-statistically significant manner. We noticed that the terms used in the conceptual models are close to those of requirements, so Advanced NLP does not have a huge impact over the results. Nonetheless, the application of the Advanced NLP techniques does not require a huge effort, and therefore its application can be deemed worthy when maximizing the quality of TLR results is a key priority.

Chapter 3

Analyzing the Impact of Natural Language Processing over Feature Location in Models

Feature Location (FL) is a common task in the Software Engineering field, specially in maintenance and evolution of software products. The results of FL depend in a great manner in the style in which Feature Descriptions and software artifacts are written. Therefore, Natural Language Processing (NLP) techniques are used to process them. Through this paper, we analyze the influence of the most common NLP techniques over FL in Conceptual Models through Latent Semantic Indexing, and the influence of human participation when embedding domain knowledge in the process. We evaluated the techniques in a real-world industrial case study in the rolling stocks domain.

3.1 Introduction

Feature Location is a common task in the Software Engineering (SE) field, specially in the maintenance and evolution of software products. The identification of Features helps with bug fixing, Feature reuse, or the formalization of Software Product Lines, amongst other tasks.

Feature Location techniques have been mainly applied to code. The results of Feature Location in code depend greatly in the style in which Feature Descriptions, code variables, and methods are written (Haiduc et al. 2013). Therefore, Natural Language Processing (NLP) techniques are used to process them, since NLP has a direct and beneficial impact on the results.

There is a wide range of NLP techniques that can be used to process text prior to Feature Location (Manning, Schütze, et al. 1999). Some of these techniques comprehend general phrase styling techniques (e.g.: lowercasing, removal of duplicate words), syntactical analysis techniques (filtering words through their role in a sentence, usually achieved through Parts-Of-Speech Tagging) (Hulth n.d.), semantic analysis techniques (filtering of words according to their meaning, usually achieved through semantic root reduction of words to their lemmas) (Plisson, Lavrac, Mladenic, et al. n.d.), and human-in-the-loop techniques (e.g.: domain terms extraction, stopwords extraction). The NLP techniques can be used independently of one another in most cases and scenarios, and are in fact combined in distinct ways by different authors depending on implementation circumstances and the particularities of their research.

For Feature Location in Conceptual Models, new techniques such as Formal Concept Analysis or Clustering have been emerging on the past years. However, the influence that NLP techniques (traditionally used for Feature Location in code) may have on Feature Location in Conceptual Models is a topic that has not received enough attention yet.

In the following pages, we present a set of custom UML Conceptual Models (described through the Background Section) from a real-world case study.

The Models differ from the code, being the elements and relationships that conform them expressed with a distinct convention and manner than the ones typically used for coding. Therefore, it is not possible to assume without further validation that the NLP techniques that are used for Feature Location in code can be immediately extrapolated with success to Feature Location in Conceptual Models.

Through this work, we aim to analyze how the usage of different combinations of NLP techniques impacts Feature Location in Models through Latent Semantic Indexing (LSI) (Landauer, Foltz, and Laham 1998; Hofmann 1999), the technique that obtains the best Feature Location results (Poshyvanyk, Gueheneuc, et al. 2007). Moreover, we elaborate on the impact of human participation over LSI results when embedding domain knowledge in the process, through the extended usage of stopwords and domain terms. We evaluated the techniques in a real-world industrial case study in the rolling stocks domain with our industrial partner, Construcciones y Auxiliar de Ferrocarriles (CAF).

Results show that using NLP techniques that achieve good results in Feature Location in code (such as Parts-Of-Speech Tagging or Lemmatizing) leads to a significant worsening of the rankings produced by LSI for Feature Location in Models. Through the Discussion of this work, we provide insight on why this is the case. For all the possible NLP combinations, embedding domain knowledge in the NLP process slightly improves the results. However, domain experts should decide whether participating in the NLP process to achieve this slight improvement is worth the effort and time involved.

The paper is structured as follows: Section 3.2 provides a background of the Models used through our work. Section 3.3 presents the Approach to our work. Section 3.4 formulates the Research Questions that we aim to respond through our work. Section 3.5 details the Experiment designed to tackle the Research Questions. Section 3.6 gives insight on the Discussion of the results of our work. Section 3.7 presents the Threats to Validity of our work. Section 3.8 summarizes the works related to the presented paper. Finally, Section 3.9 presents the conclusions of our work.

3.2 Background

This section presents the Domain Specific Language (DSL) used to formalize the Conceptual Models that implement the train control and management software of the products manufactured by our industrial partner, called Train Control Modeling Language (TCML). The TCML is a custom version of UML used by our industrial partner, that has the expressiveness required to describe both the interaction between the main pieces of equipment installed in a train unit, and the non-functional aspects related to regulation. It will be used through the rest of the paper to present a running example. For the sake of understandability and legibility, and due to intellectual property rights concerns, we present an equipment-focused simplified subset of the TCML.

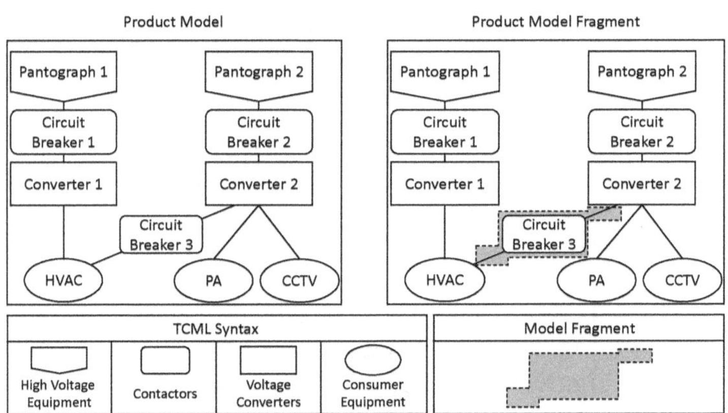

Figure 3.1: Example of Model and Model fragment

Fig. 3.1 depicts one example, taken from a real-world train. It presents a converter assistance scenario where two separate pantographs (High Voltage Equipment) collect energy from the overhead wires, and send it to their respective circuit breakers (Contactors), which in turn send it to their independent Voltage Converters. The converters then power their assigned Consumer Equipment: the HVAC on the left (the train's air conditioning system), and the PA (public address system) and CCTV (television system) on the right.

To formalize the Model fragments used by through the rest of our work, we use the Common Variability Language (CVL) (Haugen et al. 2008). The elements of Fig. 3.1 highlighted in gray conform an example Model fragment, including one circuit breaker that connects Converter 2 to a Consumer Equipment assigned to Converter 1. This Model fragment is the realization of the "converter assistance" Feature, allowing the passing of current from one converter to equipment assigned to its peer for coverage in case of overload or failure of the first one.

3.3   Approach

So far, there has been no discussion on which NLP techniques should be applied, nor on which combination (or combinations) of NLP techniques yield the best results when used to carry out Feature Location in Models. Different authors use different techniques and combinations of techniques in their research, guiding their NLP efforts through implementation circumstances and problem particularities.

The goal of the presented approach is, by targeting a real-world industrial example, to study the impact of a set of combinations of the most spread NLP techniques over a widely accepted Feature Location process, Latent Semantic Indexing (LSI). By analyzing the success of LSI over different inputs, generated through the NLP of Feature Descriptions and Models by distinct technique combinations, we aim to determine which of them guide LSI to enhanced results.

The following subsections describe the NLP techniques taken in account through the rest of this work, and the combinations of techniques that are considered for further generation of LSI results.

3.3.1   NLP Techniques

Fig. 3.2 is used here to illustrate the whole compendium of techniques considered through this work, which are detailed one by one in this section, through the following paragraphs.

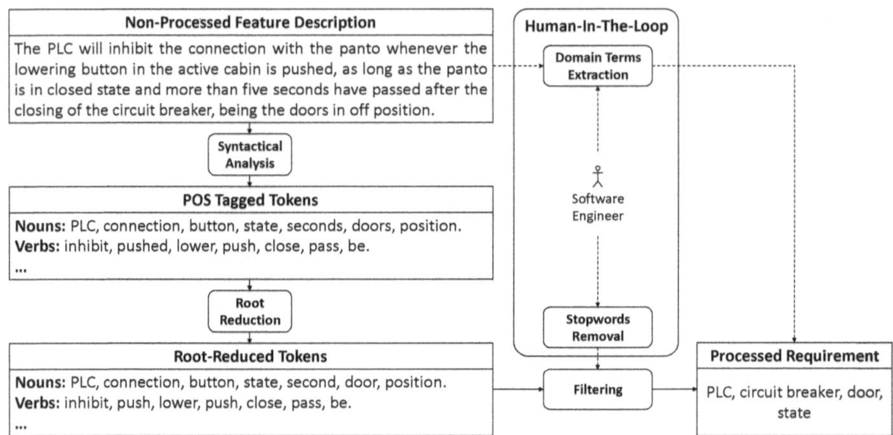

Figure 3.2: Compendium of NLP Techniques

Baseline NLP

The most basic NLP technique covered in this work is the combination of tokenizing, lowercasing, and removal of duplicate keywords, which is often used as the most basic NLP technique for several widely-known LSI examples (Garcia 2006). As such, we use it as the baseline for comparing the outcomes of the considered NLP techniques combinations. We disregard the complete lack of NLP as baseline since the scope of this work is the analysis of the outcomes of distinct NLP combinations of techniques, against verifying whether performing NLP over NL queries is better or not than not doing so.

Syntactical Analysis

Syntactical Analysis (SA) techniques split the words of NL sentences, analyzing the specific roles of each one of them in the sentence and determining their grammatical load. In other words, these techniques determine the grammatical function of each word in a particular sentence (e.g.: nouns, verbs, adjectives, adverbs, etc.).

These techniques, often referred to as Parts-Of-Speech Tagging (POS Tagging) techniques allow engineers to implement filters for words that fulfill specific grammatical roles in a sentence, usually opting for nouns, since these words are the ones that carry the relevant information about descriptions of Features and actions (Capobianco et al. n.d.). Words like verbs, adverbs, and adjectives are often filtered out and disregarded.

In Fig. 3.2, it is possible to appreciate the SA process, with the POS Tagged Tokens as outcome of syntactically analyzing a real-world NL Feature Description. Nouns and verbs are depicted while, for space reasons, the rest of the words are omitted in the Figure.

Root Reduction

Through the usage of semantic techniques such as Lemmatizing, words can be reduced to their semantic roots or lemmas. Thanks to lemmas, the language of the NL Feature Descriptions is unified, avoiding verb tenses, noun plurals, and strange word forms that interfere negatively with the Feature Location processes. Prior to carrying out Root Reduction (RR) techniques, it is imperative to use SA techniques, due to the fact that RR techniques are based on word dictionaries that are built upon the grammatical role of words in a sentence. The unification of the language semantics is an evolution over pure syntactical role filtering that allows for a more advanced filtering of words in NL Feature Descriptions.

In Fig. 3.2, it is possible to appreciate the RR process, with the Root-Reduced Tokens as outcome of the semantic analysis of the POS Tags derived from the NL Feature Description. For space reasons, only the lemmas of nouns and verbs are depicted once again.

Human-in-the-Loop

The inclusion of domain experts and, in particular, software engineers in Feature Location processes is a widely discussed topic within the SE community. It is often regarded as beneficial to have some sort of domain knowledge embedded in automated Feature Location systems, particularly on areas related to software reuse and software variability.

Some of the techniques derived from humans interacting with Feature Location processes are Domain Terms Extraction and Stopwords Removal.

In order to carry out these techniques, Software Engineers provide two separate lists of terms: one list of terms (both single-word terms and multiple-word terms) that belongs to the domain and that must be always kept for analysis, and a list of irrelevant words that can appear throughout the entirety of the specification documents and that have no value whatsoever for the analysis. Both kinds of terms can be automatically filtered in or out of the final query, depending on the needs of the domain experts.

In Fig. 3.2, it is possible to appreciate the Human-in-the-Loop process, where a software engineer provides both lists of terms, which are consequently introduced into the final query, or filtered out of it. We do not consider separating the techniques and including only one of the lists. Should we include domain knowledge in our NLP, we should benefit of the whole of it and not take out a part.

Other Filters

Many other filters can be implemented to make a NL query (in our particular case, a Feature Description written in Natural Language) suit the needs of developers and researchers alike. For instance, a technique not covered in this study is Stemming (which consists in the reduction of words to their logical root or stem through a set of logically-related grammatical rules). We opted for the inclusion of Lemmatizing on its place, due to its more precise and advanced nature on the fulfillment of the same task (Balakrishnan and Lloyd-Yemoh 2014).

3.3.2 NLP Configurations

When considering the possible configurations for the NLP techniques, we have taken in account the following facts, extracted from the prior subsection:

1 Root Reduction cannot be carried out without applying prior Syntactical Analysis.

2 We include or exclude domain knowledge as a whole.

3 The main goal of our work is to compare the distinct NLP techniques configurations, but we also aim to analyze the raw impact of embedding domain knowledge on NLP over Feature Location in Models.

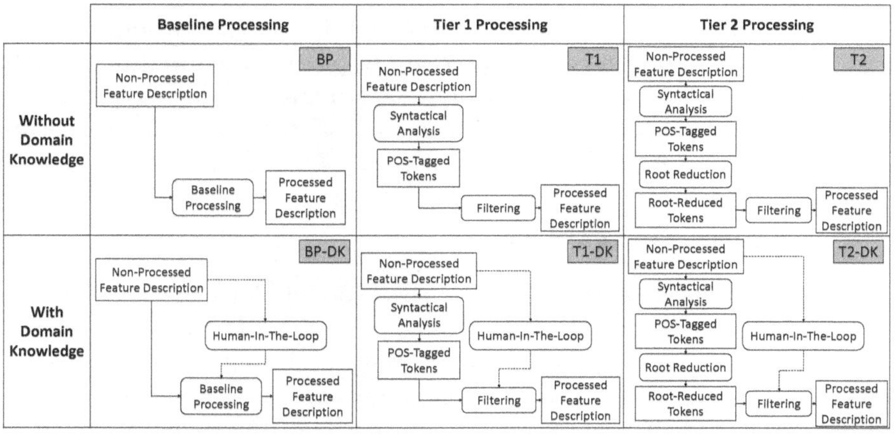

Figure 3.3: Possible NLP Techniques Configurations

Taking these three rules as our main standpoint, we have designed the table presented in Fig. 3.3.

The Figure presents tree tiers of processing (baseline processing, processing with syntactical analysis, and full processing), split in two subgroups (excluding domain knowledge, and including domain knowledge), for a total of six possible configurations:

1 Baseline Processing (**BP**).

2 Baseline Processing + Domain Knowledge (**BP-DK**).

3 Tier 1 Processing (**T1**).

4 Tier 1 Processing + Domain Knowledge (**T1-DK**).

5 Tier 2 Processing (**T2**).

6 Tier 2 Processing + Domain Knowledge (**T2-DK**).

In order to test the impact of the aforementioned configurations over the Feature Location process, we apply them to process the input of a widely used Feature Location technique, Latent Semantic Indexing (LSI). We chose LSI due to it being the technique that offers best results in Feature Location (Poshyvanyk, Gueheneuc, et al. 2007).

3.3.3 *Latent Semantic Indexing*

LSI is an automatic mathematical/statistical technique that analyzes relationships between *queries* and *documents* (bodies of text). It constructs vector representations of both a user *query* and a corpus of text *documents* by encoding them as a *term-by-document co-occurrence matrix*, and analyzes the relationships between those vectors to get a similarity ranking between the *query* and the *documents*. Through LSI, we are able to extract a ranking of the Model fragments according to their similarity to a provided query Feature Description.

First, textual representations of the Model fragments are obtained by the concatenation of the words that appear on its elements, and preprocessed with the same techniques as those used to preprocess the Feature Description.

As an example, the full Model presented in the left part of Figure 3.1, after preprocessing, would yield the textual representation "Pantograph Circuit Breaker Converter HVAC Pantograph Circuit Breaker Converter Circuit Breaker PA CCTV".

Then, the *term-by-document co-occurrence matrix* is built. *Terms* are the words that compose the preprocessed Feature Description and the preprocessed textual representation of Model fragments. *Documents* are the preprocessed textual representations of the Model fragments. Finally, the *query* is formed by one processed Feature Description. Values of *term* occurrences in both the documents and the query are counted, and used to build the *term-by-document co-occurrence matrix*. The resulting *documents* and *query* columns are then transformed into vectors, and the relationships between the *documents* and the *query* are analyzed to extract a ranking of the most similar Model fragments for the Feature Description.

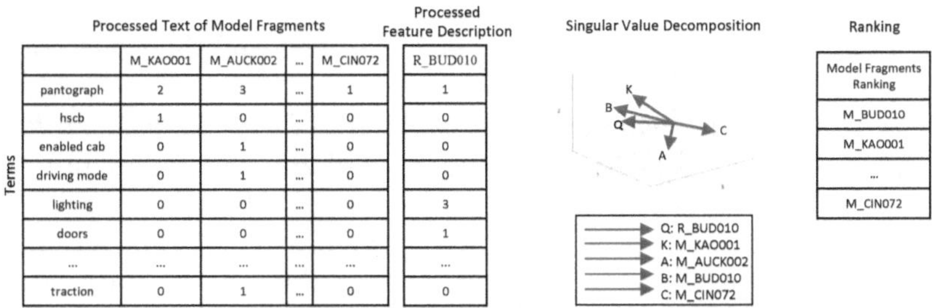

Terms	M_KAO001	M_AUCK002	...	M_CIN072	R_BUD010
pantograph	2	3	...	1	1
hscb	1	0	...	0	0
enabled cab	0	1	...	0	0
driving mode	0	1	...	0	0
lighting	0	0	...	0	3
doors	0	0	...	0	1
...	...	...	...	...	...
traction	0	1	...	0	0

Figure 3.4: Latent Semantic Indexing Example

Figure 3.4 shows an example *term-by-document co-occurrence matrix*, with values associated to our case study, the vectors, and the resulting ranking. In the following paragraphs, an overview of the elements of the matrix is provided:

- Each row in the matrix stands for each unique keyword (*term*) extracted in the first step of our approach. In Figure 3.4, it is possible to appreciate a set of representative keywords in the domain such as 'pantograph' or 'doors' as the *terms* of each row.

- Each column in the matrix stands for the preprocessed text of each Model fragment in our case study. In Figure 3.4, it is possible to appreciate the identifiers of the Model fragments in the columns such as 'M_KAO001' or 'M_CIN072', representing the preprocessed text of those Model fragments.

- The final column stands for the *query*. In our approach, the *query* column stands for the preprocessed text of a Feature Description in our case study. In Figure 3.4, the identifier of the Feature Description in the *query* column ('R_BUD010') represents its preprocessed text.

- Each cell in the matrix contains the frequency with which the *term* of its row appears in the *document* denoted by its column. For instance, in Figure 3.4, the *term* 'pantograph' appears twice in the 'M_KAO001' preprocessed text and once in the 'R_BUD010' preprocessed text.

We obtain vector representations of the *documents* and the *query* columns by normalizing and decomposing the *term-by-document co-occurrence matrix* using a matrix factorization technique called *singular value decomposition* (SVD) (Landauer, Foltz, and Laham 1998; Hofmann 1999). SVD is a form of factor analysis, or more properly the mathematical generalization of which factor analysis is a special case. In SVD, a rectangular matrix is decomposed into the product of three other matrices. One component matrix describes the original row entities as vectors of derived orthogonal factor values, another describes the original column entities in the same way, and the third is a diagonal matrix containing scaling values such that when the three components are matrix-multiplied, the original matrix is reconstructed.

In Figure 3.4, a three-dimensional graph of the SVD is provided. On the graph, it is possible to appreciate the vectorial representations of some of the matrix columns. For space reasons, only a small set of the columns is represented. In the Figure, it is possible to appreciate the B vector ('M_BUD010' vector) as the closest to the Feature Description vector, followed by vectors K, C, and A, which are the vector representations of the columns highlighted in the left part of the matrix.

To measure the similarity degree between vectors, our approach calculates the cosine between the *query* vector and the *documents* vectors. Cosine values closer to one denote a higher degree of similarity, and cosine values closer to minus one denote a lower degree of similarity. Similarity increases as vectors point in the same general direction (as more *terms* are shared between *documents*). Having this measurement, our approach orders the Model fragments according to their similarity degree to the Feature Description.

The relevancy ranking (which can be seen in Figure 3.4) is produced according to the calculated similarity degrees. In this example, LSI retrieves 'M_BUD010' and 'M_KAO001' in the first and second position of the product relevancy ranking due to the cosines being '0.9243' and '0.8454', implying a high similarity degree between the fragments and the Feature Description. On the other hand, 'M_CIN072' is returned in a latter position of the ranking due to its cosine being '-0.7836', a lower similarity degree.

3.4 Research Questions

Through this section, we aim to clearly establish what is the scope of our work, and to determine what are the research questions that we must tackle and have in mind when designing our comparison experiment. From the described problem, two research questions arise (RQ1 and RQ2), formulated in the following lines:

RQ1 How do different NLP configurations affect the efficiency and effectiveness of Feature Location in Models?

RQ2 How are human NLP efforts reflected in the outcome of Feature Location in Models?

Through the following section, we describe the experiment that we designed to address both research questions, as well as its results.

3.5   Experiment

Through the following subsections, we present our real-world case study, describe the oracle used for our experiment, detail the design of our experiment, and present the results of said experiment.

3.5.1   Case Study

We applied our experiment to a real-world case study from one of our industrial partners, CAF (Construcciones y Auxiliar de Ferrocarriles, available at   CAF is a worldwide provider of railway solutions. Their trains can be seen all over the world and in different forms (regular trains, subway, light rail, monorail, etc.).

A train unit is furnished with multiple pieces of equipment through its vehicles and cabins. These pieces of equipment are often designed and manufactured by different providers, and their aim is to carry out specific tasks for the train. Some examples of these devices are traction equipment, compressors, brakes, the pantograph that harvests power from the overhead wires, etc. The control software of the train unit is in charge of making all the equipment cooperate to achieve the train functionality, while guaranteeing compliance with the specific regulations of each country. The functionality of each train is detailed in documents where each desired Feature is specified through a Natural Language Description. In turn, the documents are implemented in Models.

For our experiment, CAF provided us with the Feature Descriptions and Models of five of their railway solutions, corresponding to the cities of Auckland, Bucharest, Cincinnati, Houston, and Kaohsiung. The trains are configured through about 100 Features per train, being each Feature described through one Feature Description. Feature Descriptions, in turn, have an average of 50 words. Regarding Models, each train is specified through no less than 8250 Model elements.

CAF also provided both a list of domain terms and a list of stopwords. The domain terms list comprehends around 300 domain terms, and the stopwords list comprehends around 60 words.

Both lists were created by a domain expert from the company with a wide knowledge of the provided software products.

3.5.2 Oracle

In order to evaluate the results of our experiment, CAF provided us with their existing documentation on Feature Location between the Feature Descriptions in the specification documents and the Models. In said documentation on Feature Location, each Feature Description is mapped to a single Model fragment. A Model fragment is a subset of elements of a Model, specified with the Model fragment formalization capacities of the Common Variability Language (CVL) (Haugen et al. 2008). In other words, for each Feature, we know which is the associated Model fragment that implements it.

We use the mapping as the oracle for evaluating the impact of each NLP techniques configuration on LSI. In order to achieve this, we analyze the results of the rankings generated by LSI, checking the position of the ranking in which the oracle (correct Model fragment for the input Feature Description) appears.

3.5.3 Design of the Experiment

In order to tackle our research questions, we need to study:

1 How Feature Location techniques respond to the different NLP inputs.

2 Whether human-introduced NLP affects the process and if so, in which manner.

To that extent, we used the aforementioned configurations of NLP techniques along with the priorly described LSI. The steps through which our experiment is performed are detailed in the following paragraphs.

The first step is to select a NLP techniques configuration. With the chosen configuration, we perform the NLP of the text of all the Feature Descriptions in our case study. The same NLP is also applied to the textual representation of all the Model fragments in our case study.

From the NLP strings, all the resulting individual words are extracted to form a list of words. The list of words (*terms*), the NLP text of the Model fragments (*documents*), and the NLP text of one Feature Description (*query*) are used as input for the LSI technique.

LSI returns a ranking of Model fragments, ordered according to the similarity between their NLP textual representation to the NLP Feature Description. Through the ranking, and by leveraging the oracle knowledge, we can determine the ranking position in which the correct Model fragment for the provided Feature Description appears.

The LSI process is performed several times, taking each of the Feature Descriptions of our case study as query, in order to extract the NLP Model fragment rankings for all the available Feature Descriptions.

Analyzing the positions in which the correct Model fragments appear, we are able to evaluate the relative success or failure in terms of results and performance of the chosen NLP techniques configuration over the LSI process.

The described steps (choosing a NLP configuration, NLP of Feature Descriptions and Model fragments, LSI, impact analysis) are carried out for the six considered configurations. By comparing the results of the six configurations, we rate their global success or failure in terms of performance and impact on the resulting rankings, and analyze the statistical impact of humans on the NLP process.

In order to perform our experiment, we used a Lenovo E330 laptop, with an Intel® Core™ i5-3210M@2.5GHz processor, with 16GB RAM and Windows 10 64-bit.

3.5.4   Statistical Analysis

To properly compare the six NLP configurations, all of the data resulting from the empirical analysis was analyzed using statistical methods following the guidelines in (Arcuri and Briand 2014).

In order to answer the RQs we perform statistical analysis to: (1) provide formal and quantitative evidence (statistical significance) that the six NLP configurations do in fact have an impact on the comparison metrics (i.e., that the differences in the results were not obtained by mere chance); and (2) show that those differences are significant in practice (effect size).

Statistical Significance

To enable statistical analysis, all of the configurations should be run a large enough number of times (in an independent way) to collect information on the probability distribution for each configuration. A statistical test should then be run to assess whether there is enough empirical evidence to claim (with a high level of confidence) that there is a difference between the two configurations (e.g., A is better than B). In order to do this, two hypothesis, the null hypothesis H_0 and the alternative hypothesis H_1, are defined. The null hypothesis H_0 is typically defined to state that there is no difference among the configurations, whereas the alternative hypotheses H_1 states that at least one configuration differs from another. In such a case, a statistical test aims to verify whether the null hypothesis H_0 should be rejected.

The statistical tests provide a probability value, $p-value$. The $p-value$ receives values ranging between 0 and 1. The lower the $p-value$ of a test, the more likely that the null hypothesis is false. It is accepted by the research community that a $p-value$ under 0.05 is statistically significant (Arcuri and Briand 2014), and so the hypothesis H_0 can be considered false.

The test that we must follow depends on the properties of the data. Since our data does not follow a normal distribution in general, our analysis requires the use of non-parametric techniques. There are several tests for analyzing this kind of data; however, the Quade test is more powerful than the rest when working with real data (García et al. 2010). In addition, according to Conover (Conover 1999), the Quade test has shown better results than the others when the number of algorithms is low, (no more than 4 or 5 algorithms).

However, with the Quade test, is not possible to answer the following question: *Which of the configurations gives the best performance?* In this case, the performance of each configuration should be individually compared against all other alternatives. In order to do this, we perform an additional post hoc analysis. This kind of analysis performs a pairwise comparison among the results of each configuration, determining whether statistically significant differences exist among the results of a specific pair of configurations. In particular, we apply the Holm Post Hoc procedure, as suggested by Garcia et al. (García et al. 2010).

Effect Size

When comparing configurations with a large enough number of runs, statistically significant differences can be obtained even if they are so small as to be of no practical value (Arcuri and Briand 2014). Then, it is important to assess if a configuration performs statistically better than another and to asses the magnitude of the improvement. *Effect size* measures are used to analyze this.

For a non-parametric effect size measure, we use Vargha and Delaney's $\hat{A}_{12}$ (Vargha and Delaney 2000; Grissom and Kim 2005). $\hat{A}_{12}$ measures the probability that using one configuration yields higher performance values than using another configuration. If the two configurations are equivalent, then $\hat{A}_{12}$ will be 0.5.

For example, $\hat{A}_{12} = 0.7$ means that we would obtain better results 70% of the times with the first of the two configurations compared, and $\hat{A}_{12} = 0.4$ means that we would obtain better results 60% of the times with the second of the two configurations. Thus, we have an $\hat{A}_{12}$ value for every pair of configurations.

3.5.5 Results

For each NLP techniques configuration, we measured the best and worst position of the oracles in the rankings generated by LSI through the steps described in the previous section, as well as the average position in which the oracle appeared. In other words, for each configuration, we measured the best, worst, and average position of the correct Model fragment in the 500 rankings generated via LSI (one ranking per available Feature Description). We also measured the time that the execution of NLP took for the different configurations (average time of 25 executions). In the table, we do not highlight the LSI execution time averages, since it is practically identical for all the configurations (around 70 seconds). The amount of time associated to create the Domain Terms and Stopwords List artifacts used to embed the Domain Knowledge along the techniques (amounting up to around 3 hours) is also neglected in the table, being a one-time event that does not account for the performance of the techniques in the long term. Table 3.1 shows the results achieved by LSI when performed over the six configurations:

Table 3.1: Results per NLP techniques configuration

	Best Result	Worst Result	Average Result	Time Taken (s)
BP	#1	#14	#5	75
BP-DK	#1	#9	#4	79
T1	#11	#26	#16	287
T1-DK	#8	#21	#13	295
T2	#5	#19	#11	342
T2-DK	#3	#12	#9	376

In the table, it is possible to appreciate that the baseline processing leads LSI to the best results, with the baseline processing with embedded domain knowledge (BP-DK) achieving slightly better results than its fully automated counterpart (BP). Both baseline processing combinations achieve a ranking position #1 as their best result, with BP-DK achieving a ranking position #9 as its worst result (improving BP's #14 in 5 positions) and improving the average result of BP by 1 position. Regarding timing, BP improves BP-DK by 4 seconds on average after 25 executions of both.

From the results, it is also possible to discern that tier one processing, in both of its forms (T1 and T1-DK), leads LSI to worse results with regards to both ranking positions and performance. The best result presented by T1 is position #11, and the worst one, #26, with the average appearance of the oracle in position #16. T1-DK improves the results of T1 in 3 positions for the best result, 5 positions for the worst result, and 3 positions on average, but its results are still nowhere near those presented by the baseline. Regarding timing, the processing performed by T1 takes 287 seconds on average after 25 executions, beating T1-DK by 8 seconds, but surpassing the best timing result (BP's) by 212 seconds.

Finally, the table shows the results obtained by LSI after applying tier two processing to Feature Descriptions and Model fragments. T2 obtains a #5 ranking position as its best result, a #19 ranking position as its worst result, and a ranking position of #11 on average. Embedding domain knowledge on tier two processing, once again, slightly improves the results of its fully automated counterpart. T2-DK obtains #3 as its best ranking position, #12 as its worst ranking position, and an average #9 position of the oracles in the rankings. From this results, it is observable that the results of tier two processing regarding ranking positions beat those of tier one processing, but are still far from those of the baseline. In addition, notice that both tier two combinations are utterly outperformed by the baseline combinations and the tier one combinations, since after 25 executions, T2 took 342 seconds and T2-DK took 376 seconds on average, which is 267 and 301 seconds slower than the best average time, respectively.

Results Statistics

The Quade test applied to the results provides $p - Values$ smaller than 0.05, which reject the null hypothesis for all the configuration pairs. Consequently, we can state that there exist differences in the configurations for the performance indicator evaluated (mean position in the ranking).

Table 3.2 shows the results of the statistical analysis performed (statistical significance and effect size).

Table 3.2: Holm's post hoc $p - Values$ and $\hat{A}_{12}$ statistic for each pair of configurations

Configurations	$p - values$	$\hat{A}_{12}$ measures
BP-DK vs BP	$4.4x10^{-5}$	0.5966
T1 vs BP	$\ll 2x10^{-16}$	0.0188
T1-DK vs BP	$\ll 2x10^{-16}$	0.0711
T2 vs BP	$\ll 2x10^{-16}$	0.1572
T2-DK vs BP	$\ll 2x10^{-16}$	0.2605
T1 vs BP-DK	$\ll 2x10^{-16}$	0
T1-DK vs BP-DK	$\ll 2x10^{-16}$	0.0183
T2 vs BP-DK	$\ll 2x10^{-16}$	0.0818
T2-DK vs BP-DK	$\ll 2x10^{-16}$	0.1628
T1-DK vs T1	$4.1x10^{-15}$	0.7082
T2 vs T1	$\ll 2x10^{-16}$	0.7962
T2-DK vs T1	$\ll 2x10^{-16}$	0.9319
T2 vs T1-DK	$4.2x10^{-13}$	0.6283
T2-DK vs T1-DK	$\ll 2x10^{-16}$	0.7976
T2-DK vs T2	$\ll 2x10^{-16}$	0.6669

The first column shows each pair of configurations, the second column shows the $p - Values$ of Holm's post hoc analysis for each pair of algorithms, and the third column shows the $\hat{A}_{12}$ statistic for each pair of configurations.

All the $p - Values$ shown in this table are smaller than their corresponding significance threshold value (0.05), indicating that the differences of performance between those configurations are significant.

Regarding the effect size, the largest differences were obtained between the T1 and BP-DK configurations (where BP-DK achieves better results than the T1 configuration 100% of times). In general, BP and BP-DK configurations obtain better results than the competitors for all the cases. When comparing BP and BP-DK, the configuration that includes Domain Knowledge (BP-DK) will produce better results around 60% of times.

3.6 Discussion

The results presented in the previous section suggest that, when faced with Feature Location in Models, the baseline processing with embedded domain knowledge guides LSI to achieving the best possible results.

The usage of more advanced techniques, on the other hand, leads to worse retrieval of results. Analyzing the Feature Descriptions, the Models, and the overall process, we noticed a series of facts that help explain why this is the case:

1 Verbs and adjectives do appear in the Models, and thus hold a vital amount of information for the Feature Location process. In addition, these words do not vary amongst Feature Descriptions and Models. For instance, verbs tend to appear always in the infinitive form (raise, open, etc.), and adjectives are invariable (electric, empty, etc.). This is not the case for nouns, which can and in fact do appear in different forms. For instance, singular and plural forms are indistinctly used through the Feature Descriptions (door vs. doors), while in the Models, it is extremely rare to find a plural form of a noun (there are only 2 occurrences of plural noun forms in the Models of the 5 trains), since multiplicity is defined through relationships between elements and not expressed in the textual representation of Models.

2 Our approach first uses POS Tagging to identify the tags of the words, and then uses said tags to filter every word out of the NLP process, except for nouns. This fact is propagated to Lemmatizing, which relies on the outcome of the filtering to perform the necessary operations to obtain the lemmas of the words. Due to the prior fact (verbs and adjectives do hold relevant information in the Models), our usage of these more complex processes removes a portion of the available information of the problem, which is useful for the Feature Location process, while the baseline does not cause this phenomena. This explains the fact that both the tier one processing and the tier 2 processing lead LSI to worse results than the baseline.

In the future, we may consider adding other tags such as verbs and adjectives to the list of words that are not to be filtered out, checking whether their inclusion can lead to Feature Location improvements.

3 As stated before, the noun words that appear in the Feature Descriptions are used in different forms in an indiscriminate manner. When performing the tier one processing, using only POS Tagging, this leads to a worsening of the results. The usage of tier two processing includes Lemmatizing, which serves as a bridge that unifies the language between the Feature Descriptions and the Model parts that are left after POS Tagging. The unification of the language is what causes the improvement that can be appreciated from tier one results to tier two results. Still, since Lemmatizing is performed after POS Tagging, a huge part of the information is already lost, and thus, the provided results do not reach the levels of those provided by the baseline. Due to this fact, we may consider testing the baseline with the inclusion of Lemmatizing in the future, while ignoring the POS Tagging filtering. We believe that, since the baseline includes nouns, it can also benefit from the language unification provided by Lemmatizing.

4 Even if we may consider testing other combinations of techniques or improving the processes through which they are being used in this work in order to test the performance of results as a case study, time performance results discourage us to use these techniques for real-world SE tasks in the environment of the company we are working with. In contrast with our reduced dataset, where the operations can be addressed in a quick and easy manner, in a real-world environment thousands of Models and Feature Descriptions must be taken in account, and the execution time of the different techniques grows exponentially. Time performance is key for the competitiveness of a company such as our industrial partner, and thus software engineers tasked with Feature Location cannot afford to wait for results for as long as some NLP techniques require. Upon revisiting the results, software engineers immediately preferred the baseline processing, since it is easier to understand, implement, and manage, as well as quicker in its execution.

This allowed them to review Model fragments and retrieve Feature Location results faster, by post-processing the given rankings through their domain knowledge and expertise.

5 We confirmed that adverbs and other connector words do not appear in the Models. Therefore, when counting occurrences of those words in the Models, the result is always zero. This leads to the fact that, by default, a percentage of the rows in the LSI term-by-document co-occurrence matrix are introduced with no information and therefore, do not contribute to the solving of the problem. A considerable percentage of these words appear in the stopwords list provided by the software engineers. The removal of these words when processing the available texts, in turn, causes the removal of their irrelevant rows from the LSI matrix. Part of the improvement caused by humans on Feature Location results is due to this fact, specially in the case of the baseline, where the inclusion of domain terms does not play a part in the improvement that can be appreciated between BP and BP-DK (see the next point for more details on this).

6 In the case of the baseline, the inclusion of domain terms does not cause a great impact on the results. After all, when using the baseline processing, all the words are included in the LSI analysis. This is not the case for POS Tagging or Lemmatizing, where the inclusion of domain terms (which are often composed, containing adjectives) causes an inclusion of information that would otherwise be discarded. On the other hand, adverbs and other connector words are discarded by POS Tagging, so the inclusion of rows with no information is a phenomena that does not occur. Looking at statements **4** and **5** altogether, we can observe that, due to the behavior of the NLP techniques, we can only benefit from one specific aspect of the domain knowledge at a time, depending on which techniques we are leveraging to guide the Feature Location process (stopwords for baseline processing, domain terms for POS Tagging based techniques).

7 Nevertheless, the evidence suggests that even though human introduced processing improves FL in all scenarios, its real impact is not significant for the results. Improving an average of 1 to 3 positions in a ranking of 500 Model fragments is not a real enhancement of FL. Domain knowledge should only be provided and embedded in NLP in cases where this is an almost immediate process. We do not recommend having software engineers employ time and effort in this task, but rather on more important, impactful duties.

These facts can be summarized as responses to our previously asked research questions:

RQ1 How do different NLP configurations affect the efficiency and effectiveness of Feature Location in Models? The baseline processing yields the best results when used to guide Feature Location in Model fragments. It outperforms more complex techniques in both results and time. More complex techniques can lead to losses of information in this field, and their execution times render them impractical in real-world scenarios.

RQ2 How are human NLP efforts reflected in the outcome of Feature Location in Models? Human NLP efforts improve the outcome of Feature Location in Model fragments in every chosen combination of techniques for different reasons, but the improvement is slight.

3.7 Threats to Validity

In this section, we use the classification of threats of validity of (Runeson and Höst 2009; Wohlin et al. 2012) to acknowledge the limitations of our approach:

1 Construct Validity: This aspect of validity reflects the extent to which the operational measures that are studied represent what the researchers have in mind. In order to minimize this risk, we study the positions of the oracles in the rankings, an objective and widely accepted measure, used before by other researchers in the community (Haiduc et al. 2013).

2 Internal Validity: This aspect of validity is of concern when causal relations are examined. There is a risk that the factor being investigated may be affected by other neglected factors. The number of Features and Models presented in this work may look small, but they implement a wide scope of different railway equipment.

3 External Validity: This aspect of validity is concerned with to what extent it is possible to generalize the finding, and to what extent the findings are of relevance for other cases. Both NL-expressed Features and Conceptual Models are frequently leveraged to specify all kinds of different software. LSI is a widely accepted and utilized technique which has proven to obtain good results in multiple domains. The NLP techniques studied through this work are also commonly used in the whole of the SE community. Therefore, our experiment does not rely on the particular conditions of our domain. Nevertheless, our findings are based on a single study. Therefore, the experiment and its results should be replicated with different kinds of models and in other domains before assuring their generalization.

4 Reliability: This aspect is concerned with to what extent the data and the analysis are dependent on the specific researchers. The Feature Descriptions and Models of the trains used through our experiment were provided by our industrial partner engineers, as well as the domain terms and stopwords lists, which were crafted by domain experts not involved in this research.

3.8   Related Work

The role of NLP is vital to the Software Engineering community (Ryan 1993). NLP has been applied to tackle different issues in software engineering at several levels of abstraction. Works like (Sultanov and Hayes 2010; Sundaram et al. 2010) or (Duan and Cleland-Huang 2007), among many others, use NLP to tackle specific problems and tasks, but do not study the implications of using different NLP techniques or combinations of techniques over the results, as our work does.

In (Falessi, Cantone, and Canfora 2013), the authors use NLP techniques to identify equivalence between NL software artifacts. The authors also define and use a series of principles for evaluating the performance of NLP when identifying said equivalence. They conclude that, in their field, the performance of NLP is determined by the properties of the given dataset over which it is performed. They measure the properties as a factor to adjust the NLP process and performance accordingly, and then apply their principles to an industrial case study. Our work differs from (Falessi, Cantone, and Canfora 2013), since the authors do not tackle the impact of different NLP configurations as we do, but rather adjust the NLP process according to a series of principles derived from dataset properties. Moreover, (Falessi, Cantone, and Canfora 2013) studies equivalence between NL software artifacts, while we analyze NLP configurations to process NL software artifacts for Feature Location in Models. In addition, we do not define a set of principles to serve as guidelines on which NLP configuration to use, but rather present the results of applying the NLP configurations to our case study, exposing the way they behave and improve (or worsen) each other. Finally, we present an in-depth study on how human involvement in the NLP process affects Feature Location in Models, an issue that (Falessi, Cantone, and Canfora 2013) does not tackle.

The work presented in (Arora et al. 2015) uses NLP to study how changes in NL software artifacts impact other artifacts of the same kind in the same specification. Through the pages of their work, the authors analyze the traceability links between NL software artifacts, and use NLP to determine how changes must propagate. Opposite to (Arora et al. 2015), our work does not analyze changes in NL software artifacts or how they affect the system. Instead, we put the focus on what is the most appropriate way of applying NLP to said artifacts for Feature Location in Models. Moreover, the authors of (Arora et al. 2015) do not consider different configurations for their NLP, but rather guide the process by taking in consideration the properties of the artifacts.

The work presented in (Eder et al. 2015) takes in consideration the possible configurations of LSI when using the technique for traceability links recovery between software artifacts, namely requirements and test cases.

In their work, the authors state that the configurations of LSI depend on the datasets used, and they look forward to automatically determining an appropriate configuration for LSI for any given dataset. In our work, we do not tackle different LSI configurations or how LSI configurations impact the results of traceability recovery between requirements and Models, but rather analyze how different NLP configurations affect the results of Feature Location in Models.

Other approaches related to the Feature Location process presented in this paper comprehend Feature and Requirement location techniques. Through the following paragraphs, we discuss said approaches and compare our work to them.

Typechef (Kästner et al. 2011) provides an infrastructure to locate the code associated to a given Feature by means of analyzing the #ifdef directives. Trace analysis (Eisenberg and Volder 2005) is a run-time technique used to locate Features. When the technique is executed, it produces traces indicating which parts of code have been executed. Some approaches related to Feature location use LSI to extract the code associated to a Feature (Poshyvanyk, Guéhéneuc, et al. 2007; Liu et al. 2007). These techniques have been generally applied to search the code of a Feature in a given individual product. The main goal of our approach, in contrast, is to analyze how NLP configurations impact Feature Location in Models.

Feature location approaches in a product family such as the one presented in (Xue, Xing, and Jarzabek 2012) center their efforts in finding the code that implements a Feature between the different products by combining techniques such as FCA (Ganter and R. Wille 2012) and LSI. In our approach, we are not interested in the code representation of a Feature in the family, but in finding the NLP configuration that guides LSI to better results when used for Feature Location in Models.

Other works such as (She et al. 2011) focus on applying reverse engineering to the source code to obtain the variability Model. In (Czarnecki and Wasowski 2007) the authors use propositional logic which describes the dependencies between Features.

In (Nadi et al. 2014) the authors combine Typechef techniques and propositional logic to extract conditions among a collection of Features. These works engage explicitly the variability of products, but do not tackle NLP configurations and their impact on Feature Location in Models, as our work does.

In (Lapeña, Ballarín, and Cetina 2016), Lapeña et al. use POS Tagging in combination with an adapted two-step LSI to obtain rankings of methods for all the requirements of a new product in a product family. The scope of the presented work, on the other hand, is centered around analyzing how distinct NLP configurations affect the results of Feature Location in Models.

Some works (D. Wille et al. 2013; Holthusen et al. 2014; Zhang, Haugen, and Møller-Pedersen 2011; Zhang, Haugen, and Møller-Pedersen 2012; Martinez et al. 2015) focus on Feature Location in Models by comparing the Models with each other to formalize the variability among them in the form of a Software Product Line. The presented work differs from these works in that the aim is not to formalize the variability, but to analyze the impact that NLP configurations have on Feature Location in Models.

Finally, Font et al. (Font et al. 2016a) use a Single Objective Evolutive Algorithm (SOEA) to locate Features among a family of Models in the form of a variation point. Their approach is refined in (Font et al. 2016b), where the authors use a SOEA to find sets of suitable Feature realizations. The authors first cluster Model fragments based on their common attributes into Feature realization candidates through Formal Concept Analysis, and then Latent Semantic Indexing ranks the candidates based on the similarity with the Feature description. The presented approach, in contrast, analyzes how NLP configurations affect Feature Location in Models.

3.9   Conclusions

Natural Language Processing (NLP) techniques have been extensively used to preprocess the language of software artifacts for Feature Location in code, due to the direct and positive impact they have on the outcome. However, the impact that these techniques have on the results of Feature Location in Models is an issue that has not been tackled yet.

Through this paper, we analyze how NLP techniques affect the outcome of Feature Location in Models. We process the Feature Descriptions and Models from a real-world industrial case study through combinations of NLP techniques, and perform Latent Semantic Indexing (LSI) over the processed specifications. We study the rankings produced by LSI with our oracle to evaluate the impact and repercussions of the NLP techniques over the Feature Location process.

Results show that using NLP techniques that have achieved good results in the past for Feature Location in code leads to a significant worsening of the rankings in the case of Feature Location in Models when compared to a Baseline Processing. We were able to identify a series of issues that cause this effect. In addition, our results highlight that embedding domain knowledge in the NLP process improves the Feature Location results, although in a non-significant manner. Domain experts should decide whether participating in the NLP process is worth the effort and time involved. The findings of our work are useful since:

1 Thanks to the retrieved results, we found out that we should not get carried away by inertia and apply NLP as we do in Feature Location in code. Advanced NLP techniques do improve the Feature Location results in the code realm, but we cannot assume that they will do so in the Models field as well. In fact, using these techniques by inertia may lead us to a worsening of the results.

2 Regarding domain experts participation in the NLP process, our results shed light on their true impact over Feature Location in Models. Thanks to that, domain experts can better value if the time and effort inverted in participating in the NLP process does pay off in terms of results improvement.

3 Finally, the Discussion of this work about NLP techniques configurations identifies specific issues that must be tackled in order to apply NLP in domains where BP-DK does not guide Feature Location in Models to proficient results.

Chapter 4

Fragment Retrieval on Models for Model Maintenance: Applying a Multi-Objective Perspective to an Industrial Case Study

Context: *Traceability Links Recovery (TLR), Bug Localization (BL), and Feature Location (FL) are amongst the most relevant tasks performed during software maintenance. However, most research in the field targets code, while models have not received enough attention yet.*

Objective: *This paper presents our approach (FROM, Fragment Retrieval on Models) that uses an Evolutionary Algorithm to retrieve the most relevant model fragments for three different types of input queries: natural language requirements for TLR, bug descriptions for BL, and feature descriptions for FL.*

__Method:__ FROM uses an Evolutionary Algorithm that generates model fragments through genetic operations, and assesses the relevance of each model fragment with regard to the provided query through a fitness configuration. We analyze the influence that four fitness configurations have over the results of FROM, combining three objectives: Similitude, Understandability, and Timing. To analyze this, we use a real-world case study from our industrial partner, which is a worldwide leader in train manufacturing. We record the results in terms of recall, precision, and F-measure. Moreover, results are compared against those obtained by a baseline, and a statistical analysis is performed to provide evidences of the significance of the results.

__Results:__ The results show that FROM can be applied in our industrial case study. Also, the results show that the configurations and the baseline have significant differences in performance for TLR, BL, and FL tasks. Moreover, our results show that there is no single configuration that is powerful enough to obtain the best results in all tasks.

__Conclusions:__ The type of task performed (TLR, BL, and FL) during the retrieval of model fragments has an actual impact on the results of the configurations of the Evolutionary Algorithm. Our findings suggest which configuration offers better results as well as the objectives that do not contribute to improve the results.

4.1 Introduction

Amongst the most common and relevant tasks in the Software Engineering field, especially when maintaining software products, are Traceability Links Recovery, Bug Localization, and Feature Location (Oliveto et al. 2010; Mahmoud, Niu, and Xu 2012; Dit et al. 2011; Rubin and Chechik 2013). To tackle these tasks, Information Retrieval (IR) techniques, such as Latent Semantic Indexing (LSI) (Landauer, Foltz, and Laham 1998; Hofmann 1999), have been used successfully (Poshyvanyk et al. 2007; Revelle, Dit, and Poshyvanyk 2010). However, most research targets code (Rubin and Chechik 2013; Dit et al. 2011; Wong et al. 2016), neglecting other software artifacts such as models. Models raise the abstraction level using concepts that are much less bound to the underlying implementation and technology and are much closer to the problem domain (Brambilla, Cabot, and Wimmer 2012). The practice of Model Driven Engineering has proved to increase efficiency and effectiveness in software development (Brambilla, Cabot, and Wimmer 2012).

To increase the automation level when Traceability Links Recovery, Bug Localization and Feature Location are performed over models, we propose an approach named Fragment Retrieval on Models (*FROM*). Our approach uses a Multi-Objective Evolutionary Algorithm to retrieve the most relevant model fragments for different types of queries (natural language requirements for Traceability Links Recovery, bug descriptions for Bug Localization, and feature descriptions for Feature Location). To guide the Evolutionary Algorithm, we use three fitness objectives: Model Similitude through Latent Semantic Indexing (LSI) (Landauer, Foltz, and Laham 1998; Hofmann 1999), Model Understandability through Model Size (Chimiak-Opoka 2011; Störrle 2014), and Model Timing through the Defect Principle (Zimmermann et al. 2004; Sisman and Kak 2012). Moreover, we combine the three objectives into a total of four configurations: (1) Similitude, (2) Similitude+Understandability, (3) Similitude+Timing, and (4) Similitude+Understandability+Timing. We analyze the impact of each configuration on the results of the Evolutionary Algorithm for Traceability Links Recovery, Bug Localization, and Feature Location.

In order to carry out this analysis, we use the models, natural language requirements, bug descriptions, and feature descriptions, all of them from a real-world case study provided by our industrial partner, Construcciones y Auxiliar de Ferrocarriles (CAF)[1], which is a worldwide leader in train manufacturing.

We record the results of the Evolutionary Algorithm for each configuration and the baseline for each type of query in terms of recall, precision, and F-measure. Also, results are compared against those obtained by a baseline in order to put FROM in perspective of previous works. The baseline retrieves model fragments using model comparisons among models instead of using an evolutionary algorithm or LSI. Our findings reveal that there is not a unique configuration of objectives that retrieves the best results for all of queries. In other words, the usage of different fitness objectives configurations is required to optimize the results of the Evolutionary Algorithm for either Traceability Links Recovery, Bug Localization, or Feature Location. In addition, we provide evidences of the significance of the results by means of statistical analysis.

The rest of the paper is structured as follows: Section 4.2 presents a motivating example. Section 4.3 presents our approach. Section 4.4 describes the evaluation, the results, and the statistical analysis. Section 4.5 discusses the results. Section 4.6 presents the threats to validity. Section 4.7 reviews the related work. Finally, Section 4.8 concludes the paper.

4.2 Motivating Example

Despite Model-Driven Development has not had the expected widespread success so far, major players in the software engineering field (i.e., tool vendors, researchers, and enterprise software developers) foresee a broad adoption of model-driven techniques because of scenarios that demand more abstract approaches than mere coding (Brambilla, Cabot, and Wimmer 2012).

Fostering modeling efforts brings benefits in industrial contexts in order to improve productivity, while ensuring quality and performance (Brambilla, Cabot, and Wimmer 2012).

In a model-driven industrial context, companies tend to have a myriad of products with large and complex models behind. The models are created and maintained over long periods of time by different software engineers, and the engineers in charge of the maintenance tasks (Traceability Links Recovery, Bug Localization, and Feature Location) often lack knowledge over the entirety of the product details. Under these conditions, maintenance tasks consume high amounts of time and effort, without guaranteeing good results. Our industrial partner reported performing the maintenance tasks manually at least 25 times per week, costing them a total monthly amount of working time ranging from 43.3 to 66.7 hours.

Figure 4.1 depicts a model example, taken from a real-world train, specified using the Domain Specific Language (DSL) that formalizes the train control and management of the products manufactured by our industrial partner. The DSL has the expressiveness required to describe both the interaction between the main pieces of installed equipment, and the non-functional aspects related to regulation. It will be used through the rest of the paper to present a running example. For the sake of understandability and legibility, and due to intellectual property rights concerns, we present an equipment-focused simplified subset of the DSL.

Specifically, the example of the figure presents a converter assistance scenario where two pantographs (High Voltage Equipment) collect energy from the overhead wires, and send it to their respective circuit breakers (Contactors), which in turn send it to their independent Voltage Converters. The converters then power their assigned Consumer Equipment: the HVAC on the left (air conditioning system), and the PA (public address system) and CCTV (television system) on the right. The elements of Figure 4.1 highlighted in gray conform an example model fragment, including one circuit breaker that connects Converter 2 to a Consumer Equipment assigned to Converter 1. This model fragment is the realization of the 'converter assistance' feature, which allows the passing of current from one converter to equipment assigned to its peer for coverage in case of overload or failure of the first converter.

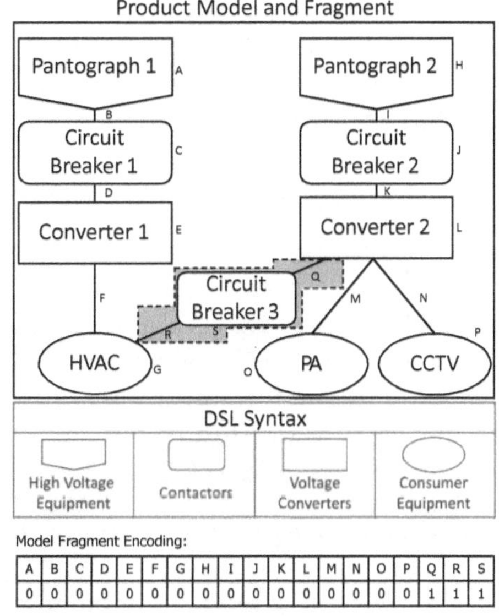

A	B	C	D	E	F	G	H	I	J	K	L	M	N	O	P	Q	R	S
0	0	0	0	0	0	0	0	0	0	0	0	0	0	0	0	1	1	1

Figure 4.1: Example of model and model fragment

A model fragment (which always belongs to a parent model) is encoded as a string of binary values that contains as many positions as elements in the parent model, where each position in the string has two possible values: 0 in case the element does not appear in the fragment, or 1 in case the element does appear in the fragment. In Figure 4.1, elements Q, R, and S conform the model fragment, so the corresponding values are set to '1' in its binary string representation.

Although it may appear easy to locate the 'converter assistance' feature in the model, it becomes very complex in the models of our industrial partner where each train unit is specified through several thousand elements. According to our industrial partner, software engineers who belonged to the original team of modelers and who work on a monthly basis with the product involved in the example, are able to locate the feature in around 26 minutes. Another engineer, not related to the project but with knowledge of the products in the company, spent 34 minutes on the same task.

Finally, two newcomer modelers spent around 40 minutes of combined work until they fulfilled the task, but they did so in a non-accurate manner. Considering these numbers, an approach that automatically retrieves model fragments is strongly needed.

4.3 Approach

The goal of the presented approach, *FROM* (Fragment Retrieval On Models), is to use an Evolutionary Algorithm to retrieve model fragments for Traceability Links Recovery, Bug Localization, and Feature Location. In addition, we use different combinations of fitness objectives as fitness function for the Evolutionary Algorithm in *FROM* in order to establish which combination of objectives guides *FROM* to the best results.

Figure 4.2 shows an overview of *FROM*. The top part of the figure highlights the inputs (the three possible types of Natural Language (NL) queries and the models where the model fragment must be retrieved), the middle part shows the steps of the Evolutionary Algorithm (including the Fitness Objectives within the Fitness Function), and the bottom part presents the four Fitness Objective Configurations considered through this work.

4.3.1 Queries

In *FROM*, we consider Traceability Links Recovery, Bug Localization, and Feature Location.

1) Traceability Links Recovery: The functionality of software products refers to what tasks a product should be able to carry out, and also to how those tasks should be carried out. It is described through specifications, which usually take the shape of NL requirements documents. The objective of Traceability Links Recovery among requirements and models is to establish the model fragment that implements a particular NL requirement. For Traceability Links Recovery, the input query is a NL requirement, for which the model fragment must be retrieved.

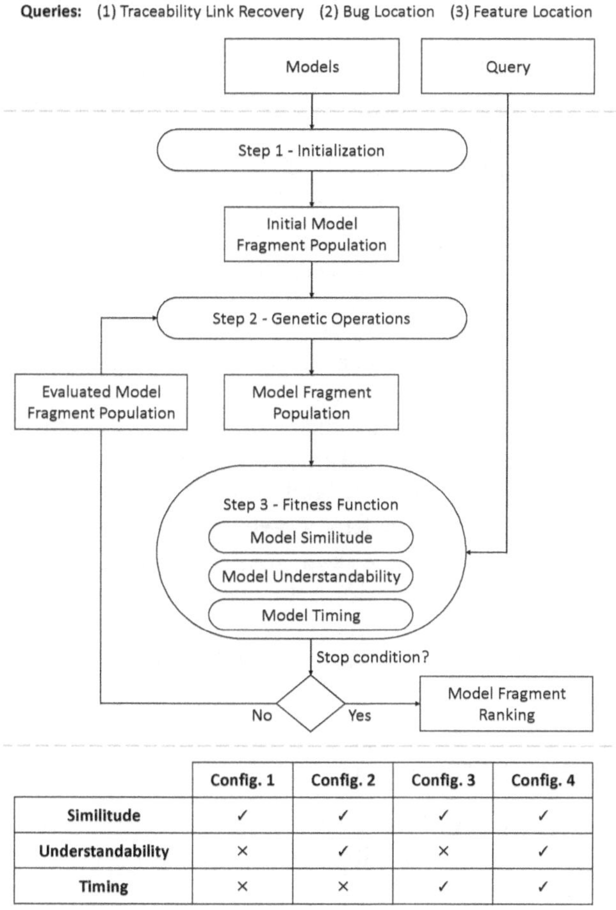

	Config. 1	Config. 2	Config. 3	Config. 4
Similitude	✓	✓	✓	✓
Understandability	✕	✓	✕	✓
Timing	✕	✕	✓	✓

Figure 4.2: Overview of the approach and configurations

For example, a functional requirement of our case study is: 'The PLC will inhibit the connection with the pantograph whenever the lowering button in the active cabin is pushed, as long as the pantograph is in closed state and more than five seconds have passed after the closing of the circuit breaker, being the doors off'.

2) Bug Localization: When errors manifest in the expected functionality of a product, software engineers create bug report documents or incidence tickets, which adopt the form of NL descriptions of the errors. The objective of Bug Localization is to identify the model fragment that causes a particular error in a product model in order to fix it. For Bug Localization, the input query is one of the error descriptions. For example, a bug description taken from our case study is: 'In case of failure of the second converter, the third converter is expected to deviate 50% of its power to the HVAC within 2 seconds, but the converter assistance scenario does not activate'.

3) Feature Location: The term 'feature' refers to a particular characteristic that a product may include. The presence or absence of a characteristic in a product, in that sense, entails the existence of different product configurations. Feature Location is concerned with identifying software artifacts (in our case, model fragments) associated with such specific characteristics. For Feature Location, the input query is the description of a feature in NL. For example, a feature taken from our case study is: 'Enabled Cabin Detection: the system will automatically determine the cabin in use through the presence of a key in the control desk, and will automatically set it as the Enabled Cabin from which the train will be controlled'.

4.3.2 Evolutionary Algorithm

Our approach relies on a Multi-Objective Evolutionary Algorithm (Fonseca, Fleming, et al. 1993) that iterates over model fragments, modifying them using genetic operations. In a previous work (Font et al. 2015), domain experts were requested to limit the search space by choosing a subset of the models, or by providing restrictions of elements that do not have to appear in the solutions. However, the search space was still very large (a model of 500 elements can yield around 10^{29} potential fragments). Evolutionary algorithms have obtained good results by addressing similar problems with large search spaces, so we have chosen to use an evolutionary algorithm. The output of the approach is a model fragment ranking for the input Traceability Links Recovery, Bug Localization, or Feature Location query. The MOEA runs in three steps:

1) Initialization: The first step of our approach is to, from the product models, generate a population of model fragments that serves as input for the genetic algorithm. In order to generate the population of model fragments, parts of the models are extracted randomly and added to a collection of model fragments.

In order to generate a random model fragment, we designed algorithm 1 (see 4.8). The algorithm first selects a random initial model element E. Then, using E, a new model fragment F is created. In addition, a second element N, neighbor to E, is taken. A valid neighbor N is an element that is directly connected to E. In case there is more than one possible neighbor element, one of the possible neighbors is randomly chosen. Then, a random number of iterations are performed.

Notice that, due to the neighbor selection process, the algorithm returns a model fragment built with a subset of elements from the parent model which are contiguously connected. This algorithm only produces fragments that are part of the original model, it does not create new elements, and the resulting model fragments keeps the conformance to the metamodel.

2) Genetic Operations: The second step of our approach is to generate a set of model fragments that could realize the provided Traceability Links Recovery, Bug Localization, or Feature Location query. The generation of new model fragments, based on existing ones, is done by applying a set of two genetic operators adapted to work over model fragments: crossover, and mutation. Both are further described in the following paragraphs.

The **crossover operation** (Font et al. 2016a) enables the creation of a new individual by combining the genetic material from two parent model fragments. The crossover operation takes the model fragment from the first parent and the model from the second parent, and generates a new individual that contains elements from both parents through model comparisons. If the comparison finds the first model fragment in the second model, the operation creates a new individual with the model fragment taken from the first parent but referencing the product model from the second parent.

Otherwise, the crossover returns the first parent unchanged. This operation broadens the search space to different models. The model fragments from the first parent and the new individual will be the same but, since parent and child can reference different models, they will often mutate differently and provide different individuals in further generations. The algorithm of this operation is outlined in Algorithm 2 (available in 4.8).

The upper part of Figure 4.3 shows an example of the application of the crossover operation. First, we select the two parents to which the operator is applied. Then, the model fragment inside the first parent is compared with the second parent. Since the comparison is able to find the model fragment in the second parent, the process creates a new individual with the model fragment, referencing the second parent.

The **mutation operator** (Font et al. 2016b) is used to imitate the mutations that randomly occur in nature when new individuals are born. That is, new individuals hold small differences with their parents that could make them adapt better (or worse) to their living environment. Following this idea, the mutation operator applied to model fragments takes as input a model fragment and mutates it into a new one, which is returned as output. As the approach is looking for fragments of a product model that realize a particular feature, the new modified fragment must remain a part of the product model. Therefore, the modifications that can be done to the model fragment must be driven by the product model.

In particular, the mutation operator can perform two distinct modifications: addition of elements to the model fragment, or removal of elements from the model fragment. To that extent, one of the two operations is firstly chosen. If the operation 'addition' is chosen (see the bottom-left part of Figure 4.3), an element of the fragment with connections to model elements that are not included in the fragment is chosen in order to add one of these non-included model elements to the fragment. For instance, the *Converter 1* element of the fragment has a connection with the *HVAC* model element, not included in the original model fragment. As result of the addition operation, a modified model fragment that includes the *HVAC* model element is obtained.

If the operation 'removal' is chosen (see the bottom-right part of Figure 4.3), an element of the model fragment that is connected with only one other element of the model fragment is chosen to be removed from the model fragment. For instance, a modified model fragment that does not include the Pantograph 1 model element is obtained as a result of the removal operation. The algorithm of this operation is outlined in Algorithm 3 (available in 4.8).

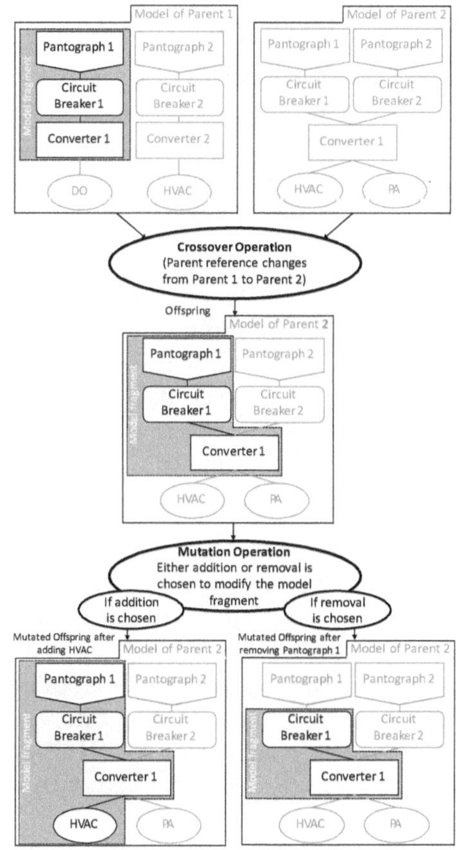

Figure 4.3: Genetic operations example

3) Fitness Function: The third step of the approach assesses each of the produced candidate model fragments, ranking them according to a fitness function. Our approach presents fitness functions based on combinations of three distinct fitness objectives, detailed in the following section.

4.3.3 Fitness Objectives

In this section, details are provided for each objective.

1) Model Fragment Similitude: To assess the relevance of each model fragment with relation to the provided query, we apply methods based on Information Retrieval (IR) techniques. In particular, we apply Latent Semantic Indexing (LSI) (Landauer, Foltz, and Laham 1998; Hofmann 1999) to analyze the relationships between the model fragments in the population and the query.

However, results retrieved by LSI depend greatly on the style on which the Natural Language (NL) of the input is written. It is often regarded as beneficial to preprocess the inputs of LSI through Natural Language Processing (NLP) techniques (Haiduc et al. 2013) to improve LSI results. A frequent practice to achieve said preprocessing is to use a combination of Parts-of-Speech (POS) tagging, removal of stopwords, and stemming, as presented in (Hulth 2003).

In our approach, we adopt said practice to process the NL from the model fragments and the queries. The NL texts of both the model fragments and the queries are preprocessed through the following steps: (1) our approach searches for domain terms provided by the software engineers in the text, saving them; (2) POS tagging is applied to the text, and the POS tags of the words are analyzed and filtered by their syntactic role, keeping only the nouns, as suggested by (Hulth 2003); and (3) the remaining POS Tags are stemmed, and refined with a set of stopwords, also provided by the software engineers. The stemmed POS Tags from Step 3 plus the saved domain terms from Step 1 build the text of the processed elements used as input for LSI.

Once the NL texts from both the model fragments and the query are processed, it is possible to apply the LSI technique. LSI constructs vector representations of a query and a corpus of text documents by encoding them as a term-by-document co-occurrence matrix. That is, a matrix where each row corresponds to *terms* and each column corresponds to *documents*, followed by the *query* in the last column. Each cell of the matrix holds the number of occurrences of a *term* inside a *document* or the *query*. In our approach, *terms* are all the individual words from the processed NL of model fragments and the query, the *documents* are the NL representations of model fragments, and the *query* is the provided Traceability Links Recovery, Bug Localization, or Feature Location query. To generate the *documents*, the model fragments are processed to extract the terms that correspond to the elements that conforms them. The words obtained this way for a particular model fragment conform its corresponding *document*.

Once the matrix is built, it is normalized and decomposed into a set of vectors using a matrix factorization technique called Singular Value Decomposition (SVD) (Landauer, Foltz, and Laham 1998). SVD is a form of factor analysis, or more properly the mathematical generalization of which factor analysis is a special case. In SVD, a rectangular matrix is decomposed into the product of three other matrices. One component matrix describes the original row entities as vectors of derived orthogonal factor values, another describes the original column entities in the same way, and the third is a diagonal matrix containing scaling values such that when the three components are matrix-multiplied, the original matrix is reconstructed. In SVD, a 'k' value of dimensions is chosen as a tuning parameter, reducing the matrices accordingly. According to recent research, keeping a 'k' value of around 300 (or the maximum, if there are less than 300 dimensions) will usually provide the best possible results with moderate-sized document collections (Bradford 2008). However, as stated by (Thomas et al. 2013) and (Borg, Runeson, and Ardö 2014), the 'k' value should be studied and tuned for each approach individually in order to optimize the results. In their work, Khatiwada et al. (Khatiwada, Tushev, and Mahmoud 2018) determine the 'k' parameter through a brute force strategy, generating several 'k' values and evaluating the performance of each of their datasets for every 'k' value.

The tuning of the 'k' parameter for our work, however, is out of the scope of this paper, and as such we acknowledge it as future work.

Using SVD, one vector that represents the latent semantics of the NL texts is obtained for each *document* and for the *query*. Finally, the similarities between each *document* and the *query* are calculated as the cosine between both of their vectors, obtaining values between -1 and 1.

The top part of Figure 4.4 shows an example of co-occurrence matrix, taken from our approach (for space reasons, columns and rows are shown in a compact way). Each *document* column is a NL representation of one of the model fragments in the population. The *query* column is the provided input Traceability Links Recovery, Bug Localization, or Feature Location query. Each *term* row is one of the words extracted from the NL texts of model fragments and the provided Traceability Links Recovery, Bug Localization, or Feature Location query. Each cell shows the number of occurrences of each of the *terms* in the model fragments. The bottom left part of Figure 4.4 shows the result of applying the SVD technique to the matrix. The vector labeled with 'Q' represents the *query*, while the ones labeled as 'MF' represent *document* model fragments. Bottom right part of Figure 4.4 shows the scores of each model fragment, calculated by computing the cosine between their associated vector and the *query* vector.

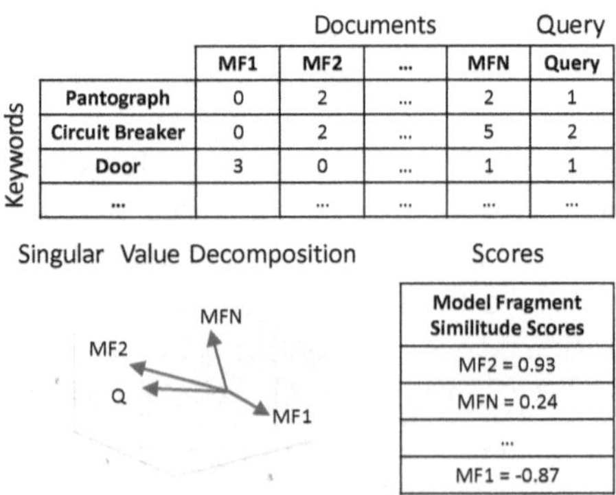

Figure 4.4: LSI example

2) Model Fragment Understandability. There are several metrics that measure different factors in models, such as their underlying complexity or their understandability by humans (Chimiak-Opoka 2011). The findings published in (Störrle 2014) prove that there is a strong correlation between the size of a particular model and its understandability by a human modeler, therefore impacting the performance of the modeler when working with it. When presented with several models for an industrial solution, smaller models always entail better modeler performance results.

To measure the size of a model fragment, three metrics are defined in (Störrle 2014) and described in 4.8: **U1**) Counting the number of elements in a model, **U2**) Weight factors per model element, and **U3**) Weight factors per model element per diagram type.

In (Störrle 2014), the author analyzes the results of applying the three metrics to a set of models, finding that the three metrics are extremely correlated, with none yielding significantly better results over the other two. Since it is easier to implement and compute, it is strongly suggested to use **U1**. Therefore, we use **U1** as the metric of choice for our Understandability Fitness Objective.

3) Model Fragment Timing. The Defect Principle, or Defect Localization Principle, states that the most recent modifications to a project are the most relevant for certain Information Retrieval purposes (Hassan and Holt 2005; Zimmermann et al. 2004; Sisman and Kak 2012). Through the Defect Principle, modification timespans can be considered and introduced as a Fitness Objective for Traceability Links Recovery, Bug Localization, and Feature Location.

Through this work, we carry out Traceability Links Recovery, Bug Localization, and Feature Location on models. Therefore, our aim is to retrieve the most relevant model fragments for a particular Traceability Links Recovery, Bug Localization, or Feature Location query. Model fragments are formed by model elements, and each model element has an associated modification time. When we apply the Defect Principle to model fragments, we have to decide how to assign a modification time to the model fragment from the modification time information on its model elements.

There are four possible measurements of the modification timespans for the Defect Principle:

(1) **Most recent model modifications:** this measurement captures the modification timespan of the most recently modified model element.

(2) **Oldest model modifications:** this measurement captures the modification timespan of the least recently modified model element.

(3) **Mean of the modification timespan of the modified model elements:** the value of the measurement is the mean value of the modification timespans of the model elements.

(4) **Sum of the modification timespan of the modified model elements:** the value of the measurement is the sum of the modification timespans of the model elements.

Software engineers from our industrial partner, when faced with different model fragments, declared that those they had modified more recently were more familiar to them, thus easier to understand and work with. Therefore, we chose measurement (1) as the way to evaluate our Model Timing Fitness Objective.

The time difference is based on the number of days and can therefore be very large when the model fragment was modified a long time ago. To normalize the time difference, mathematical solutions such as square root or logarithm can be used. We used square roots because it has achieved good results in other works that use time differences (Zimmermann et al. 2004).

Figure 4.5 shows an example of timespan for each model element of the model fragment highlighted in gray. For example, the *Circuit Breaker 1* has been modified 89 days ago. Since the most recent model modification is 17 days (from the *Convert1* model element), the value of the model fragment is 17 days that means a square root of 4.123.

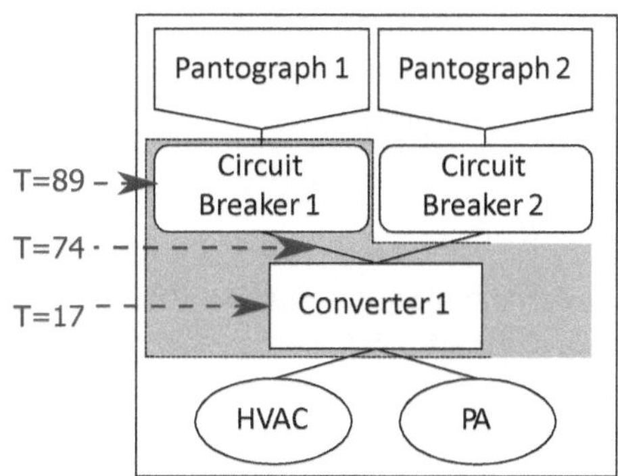

Figure 4.5: Timespan of the modifications of the model elements of a fragment

4.3.4 Fitness Objectives Configurations

To compare how the distinct objective configurations affect *FROM* for the different types of queries, we have designed a total four possible objective configurations (shown in the bottom part of Figure 4.2):

C1: Similitude.

C2: Similitude + Understandability.

C3: Similitude + Timing.

C4: Similitude + Understandability + Timing.

It is worth mentioning that creating configurations without the Similitude measurement is possible, but meaningless. Such configurations would produce the smallest and/or most recently modified model fragments in the case study, regardless on whether they had anything to do with the introduced query, rendering them useless.

4.4 Evaluation

This section presents the evaluation of our approach.

4.4.1 Research Questions

There are several aspects that we want to evaluate with regard to how the different configurations affect FROM for the different types of queries. In order to address the evaluation of these aspects, we formulated the following research questions:

RQ$_1$: *How does the performance of the different objective configurations compare to the performance of the baseline for different query types?*

RQ$_2$: *Is the difference in performance between the objective configurations and the baseline significant?*

RQ$_3$: *Does the type of query have an impact on the performance of the different objective configurations?*

4.4.2 Baseline

In order to put the performance of *FROM* in perspective and to relate our work to previous works, we compare it to a baseline for fragment retrieval in models. Traditionally, fragment retrieval in models has been performed through model comparisons among models (D. Wille, Sönke Holthusen, et al. 2013a; Sönke Holthusen et al. 2014a; X. Zhang, Øystein Haugen, and Moller-Pedersen 2011; X. Zhang, Ø. Haugen, and Møller-Pedersen 2012; Jabier Martinez et al. 2015a; J. Martinez et al. 2015). These works classify the elements based on their similarity and identify the dissimilar elements as the model fragments. The predominant technology of choice to implement their approaches is EMF Model Compare, which relies on Model Matching to perform the comparisons. Hence, the baseline is our implementation of the algorithms to retrieve fragments presented in (X. Zhang, Øystein Haugen, and Moller-Pedersen 2011), which also uses EMF Model Compare to perform the model comparisons as the previous works.

4.4.3 Experimental Setup

FROM and the baseline are executed taking as input the query and the models provided by our industrial partner. Our industrial partner provided us with: 103 natural language requirements, 121 feature descriptions and 42 bug descriptions of their railway solutions. The models of 23 trains are specified through an average of 8250 model elements.

We executed 30 independent runs for each query and approach (the four configurations of *FROM* and the baseline) for *FROM* (as suggested by (Arcuri and Fraser 2013)), i.e., 103 (natural language requirements) x 5 (approaches) x 30 repetitions + 121 (feature descriptions) x 5 (approaches) x 30 repetitions + 42 (bug descriptions) x 5 (approaches) x 30 repetitions = 39900 independent runs.

Once the four configurations of *FROM* and the baseline are executed, we obtain as result a ranking of model fragments. Next, we take the best solution of the ranking (the model fragment at position 1) to compare it with an oracle, which is the ground truth. Once the comparison is performed, a confusion matrix is calculated.

A confusion matrix is a table often used to describe the performance of a classification model on a set of test data (the best solutions) for which the true values are known (from the oracle). In our case, each solution obtained is a model fragment composed of a subset of the model elements that are part of the product model. Since the granularity is at the level of model elements, each model element presence or absence is considered as a classification. The confusion matrix distinguishes between the predicted values and the real values classifying them into four categories:

- True Positive (TP): values that are predicted as true (in the solution) and are true in the real scenario (the oracle).

- False Positive (FP): values that are predicted as true (in the solution) but are false in the real scenario (the oracle).

- True Negative (TN): values that are predicted as false (in the solution) and are false in the real scenario (the oracle).

- False Negative (FN): values that are predicted as false (in the solution) but are true in the real scenario (the oracle).

Then, some performance measurements are derived from the values in the confusion matrix. In particular, we create a report including three performance measurements: recall, precision, and F-measure for the baseline and configurations for each type of query.

Recall measures the number of elements of the solution that are correctly retrieved by the proposed solution and is defined as follows:

$$Recall = \frac{TP}{TP + FN}$$

Precision measures the number of elements from the solution that are correct according to the ground truth (the oracle) and is defined as follows:

$$Precision = \frac{TP}{TP + FP}$$

F-measure corresponds to the harmonic mean of precision and recall and is defined as follows:

$$F - measure = 2 * \frac{Precision * Recall}{Precision + Recall}$$

Recall values can range between 0% (no single model element obtained from the oracle is present in any of the model fragments of the solution) to 100% (all the model elements from the oracle are present in the solution). Precision values can range between 0% (no single model fragment from the solution is present in the oracle) to 100% (all the model fragments from the solution are present in the oracle). A value of 100% precision and 100% recall implies that both the solution and the oracle are the same.

At this point, it is important to highlight that the fitness objective Configuration 1 (Similitude) is a Single-Objective Evolutionary Algorithm (SOEA), whereas the other three configurations are MOEA. For this reason, other common MOEA measures such as hypervolume (Zitzler and Thiele 1998) are not necessarily suitable for comparing solutions by MOEAs with solutions by SOEAs as the work in (Ishibuchi, Nojima, and Doi 2006) shows.

Therefore, in order to compare the results, we first take the best solution of Configuration 1 for its single-objective (similitude with the query). Second, we take the best solution of each of the other configurations with regard to the objective of Configuration 1 (similitude with the query) as described in (Ishibuchi, Nojima, and Doi 2006).

4.4.4 Oracle Preparation

The oracle was provided by our industrial partner, since the model fragments that realize each of the 103 requirements, 121 features and 42 bugs were already documented. It is also worth noting that the oracle has not been created for this evaluation, and that many of the provided model fragments were created by engineers who are currently not working in the company. We checked both that there were no queries without model fragments, and that the model fragments were in the models provided for the evaluation.

4.4.5 Implementation Details

FROM[2] is based on NSGA-II (Deb et al. 2002), one of the most frequently used Multi-Objective Evolutionary Algorithms. Given a population of model fragments where each model fragment has up to three fitness values (see Subsection 4.3.4), NSGA-II orders these model fragments by means of non-dominated sorting. A model fragment is non-dominated when there is no other model fragment that improves any fitness value without worsening other fitness value. As a result, NSGA-II finds pareto-optimal model fragments.

The rest of the settings such as population size, crossover probability, and mutation probability are detailed in Table 4.1. For those settings, we have chosen values that are commonly used in the literature (Sayyad et al. 2013). The values are 100, 0.9, and 0.1, respectively.

Table 4.1: Parameter settings

Parameter description	Value
Size: Population Size	100
μ: Number of Parents	2
λ: Number of offspring from μ parents	2
r: Solutions replaced at population size	2
$p_{crossover}$: Crossover probability	0.9
$p_{mutation}$: Mutation probability	0.1

In general, there are two atomic performance measures for evolutionary algorithms: one regarding solution quality and one regarding algorithm speed or search effort. In this paper, we focus on the solution quality (i.e., obtaining a solution that is more similar to the one from the oracle in terms of precision and recall). After running some prior tests for each fitness configuration to determine the time to converge (and adding a margin to ensure convergence), we allocated a fixed amount of wall clock time (80 seconds) to stop the execution. During that time, our algorithm is capable of executing an average of 7307 generations (with an standard deviation of 1500 generations). We performed the execution of FROM using an array of computers with processors ranging from 4 to 8 cores, clock speeds between 2.2 GHz and 4GHz, and 4-16 GB of RAM. All of them were running Windows 10 Pro N 64 bits as the hosting Operative System and the Java(TM) SE Runtime Environment (build 1.8.0 73-b02).

We have used the Eclipse Modeling Framework to manipulate the models and the Common Variability Language (CVL) (Øystein Haugen et al. 2008) to manage the model fragments. The NLP techniques used to process the language have been implemented using OpenNLP (Apache 2016) for the POS Tagger (accounting for an 88% precision (Horsmann, Erbs, and Zesch 2015)) and the English (Porter 2) (Porter 2016) stemming algorithm. LSI has been implemented using the Efficient Java Matrix Library (Abeles n.d.). The genetic operations are built upon the Watchmaker Framework for Evolutionary Computation (Dyer 2016).

The available implementation presented in FROM is limited by confidentiality agreements in force with our industrial partner, since the approach is currently in use, and the trains of the case study are currently operating and under maintenance contracts.

4.4.6 Research Question 1

To answer how is the performance of the configurations and the baseline, this subsection presents the results of performance. Figure 4.6 shows the charts with the recall and precision results for the configurations and the baseline (rows of the figure) and the type of query (columns in the figure). A dot in the graphs represents the average result of recall and precision for the 30 repetitions.

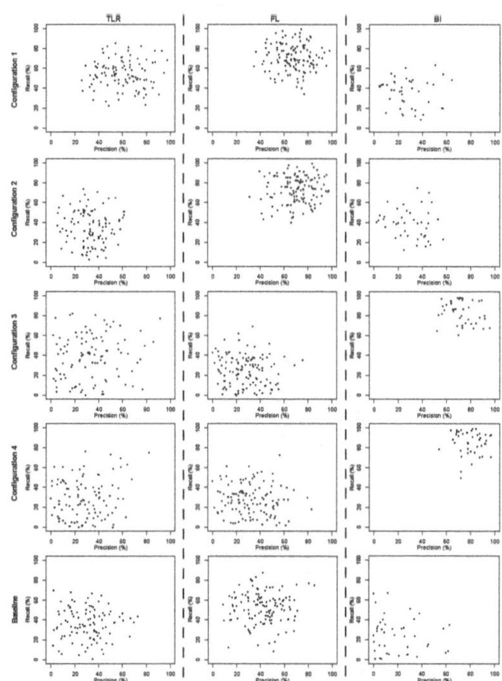

Figure 4.6: Mean Recall and Precision values for *FROM* and the baseline

RQ$_1$ answer. Table 4.2 shows the mean values of recall, precision and F-measure of the graphs for the four configurations and the baseline (rows) in Traceability Links Recovery, Feature Location and Bug Localization (columns).

In Traceability Links Recovery, Configuration 1 obtains the best results in recall and precision, providing and average value of 54.33% in recall and 59.93% in precision.

In Feature Location, Configuration 2 obtains the best results in recall and precision, providing and average value of 73.29% in recall and 70.60% in precision.

In Bug Localization, Configuration 4 obtains the best results in recall and precision, providing and average value of 84.91% in recall and 79.94% in precision.

Table 4.2: Mean Values and Standard Deviations for Recall, Precision and F-Measure

	Recall $\pm$ (σ)		
	TLR	FL	BL
Configuration 1	54.33±14.23	70.95±13.59	35.95±14.49
Configuration 2	35.21±17.05	73.29±13.65	39.47±14.73
Configuration 3	38.72±22.14	25.04±15.06	83.09±11.28
Configuration 4	29.07±19.66	27.85±15.05	84.91±11.85
Baseline	36.14±15.55	58.20±15.66	24.87±17.81
	Precision $\pm$ (σ)		
	TLR	FL	BL
Configuration 1	59.93±16.94	67.68±13.43	28.12±15.45
Configuration 2	33.69±13.69	70.60±14.08	30.54±14.91
Configuration 3	33.93±20.85	27.97±15.22	72.77±11.19
Configuration 4	29.10±17.84	32.81±17.37	79.94±10.19
Baseline	30.99±16.25	41.90±16.16	20.13±18.61
	F-measure $\pm$ (σ)		
	TLR	FL	BL
Configuration 1	54.87±11.61	67.87±9.82	27.55±12.13
Configuration 2	30.62±12.49	70.67±10.78	30.51±12.43
Configuration 3	30.27±18.24	21.50±12.17	76.62±7.13
Configuration 4	23.51±16.50	25.38±12.52	81.59±8.15
Baseline	29.39±12.94	45.98±13.44	15.09±12.36

4.4.7 Research Question 2

To answer whether there are significant differences in performance among the different configurations of our *FROM* approach and the baseline in Traceability Links Recovery, Feature Location, and Bug Localization, the results should be properly compared. To do this, all of the data resulting from the empirical analysis was analyzed using statistical methods following the guidelines in (Arcuri and Briand 2014).

The goals of our statistical analysis are: (1) to provide formal and quantitative evidence (statistical significance) that the configurations and the baseline do in fact have an impact on the comparison metrics (i.e., that the differences in the results were not obtained by mere chance); and (2) to show that those differences are significant in practice (effect size).

To enable statistical analysis, all configurations should be run a large enough number of times (independently) to collect information on the probability distribution for each type of query. A statistical test should then be run to assess whether there is enough empirical evidence to claim that there is a difference between the two configurations. In order to do this, two hypotheses are defined: (1) the null hypothesis H_0 is typically defined to state that there is no difference among the configurations and the baseline, and (2) the alternative hypothesis H_1 states that at least one configuration differs from another. A statistical test aims to verify whether H_0 should be rejected.

The statistical tests provide a probability value, $p-value$, which obtains values between 0 and 1. The lower the $p-value$ of a test, the more likely that H_0 is false. It is accepted by the research community that a $p-value$ under 0.05 is statistically significant (Arcuri and Briand 2014), and so H_0 can be considered false.

The test to follow depends on the properties of the data. Since our data does not follow a normal distribution, our analysis requires the use of non-parametric techniques. There are several tests for analyzing this kind of data; however, the Quade test shows is more powerful when working with real data (García et al. 2010).

In addition, according to Conover (Conover 1999), the Quade test has shown better results than the others when the number of algorithms is low (no more than 4 or 5 algorithms).

RQ$_2$ answer. The $p - Values$ and statistics of the Quade test are shown in the upper part of Table 4.3. Since the $p - Values$ shown in this table are smaller than 0.05 in all cases, we reject the null hypothesis. Consequently, we can state that there are significant differences in the configurations and the baseline of Traceability Links Recovery, Feature Location and Bug Localization for all the performance indicators (recall and precision).

Table 4.3: Results of the statistical analysis

| | Quade test statistic and $p - Values$ | | | | | |
| | Traceability Links Recovery | | Feature Location | | Bug Localization | |
	Recall	Precision	Recall	Precision	Recall	Precision
$p - value$	$5.0x10^{-16}$	$\ll 2.2x10^{-16}$	$\ll 2.2x10^{-16}$	$\ll 2.2x10^{-16}$	$\ll 2.2x10^{-16}$	$\ll 2.2x10^{-16}$
Statistic	21.38	40.42	145.06	110.99	60.81	63.24

| | Holm's post hoc $p - Values$ | | | | | |
| | Traceability Links Recovery | | Feature Location | | Bug Localization | |
	Recall	Precision	Recall	Precision	Recall	Precision
C1 vs C2	$2.7x10^{-15}$	$\ll 2x10^{-16}$	0.2	0.15	0.26	0.33
C1 vs C3	$2.7x10^{-08}$	$\ll 2x10^{-16}$	$\ll 2x10^{-16}$	$\ll 2x10^{-16}$	$3.1x10^{-14}$	$3.1x10^{-14}$
C1 vs C4	$\ll 2x10^{-16}$	$\ll 2x10^{-16}$	$\ll 2x10^{-16}$	$\ll 2x10^{-16}$	$4.1x10^{-14}$	$4.1x10^{-14}$
C1 vs Baseline	$4.3x10^{-16}$	$\ll 2x10^{-16}$	$2x10^{-10}$	$\ll 2x10^{-16}$	0.002	0.025
C2 vs C3	0.27	0.8	$\ll 2x10^{-16}$	$\ll 2x10^{-16}$	$9.4x10^{-14}$	$3.1x10^{-14}$
C2 vs C4	0.02	0.03	$\ll 2x10^{-16}$	$\ll 2x10^{-16}$	$4.1x10^{-14}$	$3.1x10^{-14}$
C2 vs Baseline	0.73	0.26	$2.4x10^{-15}$	$\ll 2x10^{-16}$	$9.9x10^{-05}$	0.005
C3 vs C4	0.002	0.15	0.22	0.03	0.28	0.003
C3 vs Baseline	0.36	0.52	$\ll 2x10^{-16}$	$9.6x10^{-12}$	$3.1x10^{-14}$	$5.4x10^{-14}$
C4 vs Baseline	0.002	0.46	$\ll 2x10^{-16}$	$6.6x10^{-05}$	$3.1x10^{-14}$	$3.1x10^{-14}$

| | $\hat{A}_{12}$ statistic for each pair | | | | | |
| | Traceability Links Recovery | | Feature Location | | Bug Localization | |
	Recall	Precision	Recall	Precision	Recall	Precision
C1 vs C2	0.7982	0.8811	0.4456	0.4358	0.4563	0.4388
C1 vs C3	0.7105	0.8312	0.9868	0.9701	0.0006	0.0130
C1 vs C4	0.8433	0.8893	0.9807	0.9381	0.0045	0.0028
C1 vs Baseline	0.8024	0.8873	0.7275	0.8867	0.7018	0.6590
C2 vs C3	0.4487	0.5212	0.9905	0.9736	0.0130	0.0040
C2 vs C4	0.6040	0.5932	0.9839	0.9473	0.0130	0.0005
C2 vs Baseline	0.4812	0.5554	0.7639	0.9066	0.7415	0.6910
C3 vs C4	0.6284	0.5613	0.4555	0.4198	0.4453	0.3226
C3 vs Baseline	0.5378	0.5277	0.0678	0.2653	0.9972	0.9858
C4 vs Baseline	0.3793	0.4627	0.0890	0.3474	0.9949	0.9977

4.4.8 Research Question 3

To answer whether a configuration has a significant impact in performance, the performance of the configuration should be statistically compared against all others. In order to do this, we perform an additional post hoc analysis (pair-wise comparison among configurations, also including the baseline). The middle part of Table 4.3 shows the $p-Values$ of Holm's post hoc analysis for pair-wise comparison of configurations and the baseline for the performance indicators in Traceability Links Recovery, Feature Location and Bug Localization. The majority of the $p-Values$ shown in this table are smaller than their corresponding significance threshold value (0.05), indicating that the differences of performance between the configurations are significant. However, some values are greater than the threshold, indicating that the differences between those configurations are not significant.

However, when comparing configurations with a large enough number of runs, statistically significant differences can be obtained even if they are so small as to be of no practical value (Arcuri and Briand 2014). It is important to assess, through *effect size* measures, if a configuration is statistically better than another one, and if so, the magnitude of the improvement.

For a non-parametric effect size measure, we use Vargha and Delaney's $\hat{A}_{12}$ (Vargha and Delaney 2000; Grissom and J. J. Kim 2005). $\hat{A}_{12}$ measures the probability that running one configuration yields higher values than running another configuration. If the two configurations are equivalent, then $\hat{A}_{12}$ will be 0.5. For example, $\hat{A}_{12} = 0.7$ means that the first of the pair of configurations would obtain better results in 70% of the runs, and $\hat{A}_{12} = 0.3$ means that the second of the pair of configurations would obtain better results in 70% of the runs. We record an $\hat{A}_{12}$ value for every pair of configurations as well as for every configuration and the baseline in Traceability Links Recovery, Feature Location and Bug Localization.

The lower part of Table 4.3 shows the values of the effect size statistics between the configurations and the baseline in Traceability Links Recovery, Feature Location and Bug Localization.

In Traceability Links Recovery, the largest differences were obtained in comparisons that entail Configuration 1, where the largest difference is obtained when compared with Configuration 4 (0.8433 for recall and 0.8893 for precision). Therefore, Configuration 1 outperforms Configuration 4 for recall and precision with a pronounced superiority (84.33% of the times for recall and 88.93% of the times for precision). In Feature Location, Configuration 1 and Configuration 2 show a pronounced superiority over Configuration 3, Configuration 4 and the baseline. The largest difference is obtained when comparing Configuration 2 with Configuration 3 (0.9905 for recall and 0.9736 for precision). In Bug Localization, Configuration 3 and Configuration 4 show a pronounced superiority over Configuration 1 and Configuration 2. The largest differences are obtained when comparing Configuration 1 with Configuration 3 for recall (0.0006) and when comparing Configuration 2 with Configuration 4 for precision (0.0005).

RQ$_3$ answer. From the results, we can conclude that the configuration against the type of query has an actual impact in performance.

4.5   Discussion

The results of our approach show that the configuration of fitness objectives that provides the best result in Traceability Links Recovery, Bug Localization and Feature Location is different for each of them. As described in Section 4.4.5, the parameters of the evolutionary algorithm in use have been chosen according to the literature values. However, as suggested by (Arcuri and Fraser 2013) and confirmed in (Kotelyanskii and Kapfhammer 2014), tuned parameters can outperform default values, but are far from optimal in individual problem instances. Since the objective of this paper is to evaluate the different configurations, we do not tune the values to improve the performance of our algorithm.

By analyzing the impact on the results for Traceability Links Recovery, Bug Localization and Feature Location of the four configurations of fitness objectives, our findings suggest that:

1 From the four configurations, there is not a unique combination of objectives that retrieves the best results for all the types of queries.

2 Model Similitude, by itself, obtains the best results in the queries for Traceability Links Recovery but it is not powerful enough to achieve the best results in the queries for Feature Location and Bug Location.

3 Model Understandability, which is a desirable objective (since it allows for an easier comprehension of model fragments by software engineers) cannot be systematically applied to Traceability Links Recovery. The configurations where it is applied (2 and 4) yield worse Traceability Links Recovery results than those where it is not applied.

4 Model Timing is only useful for Bug Localization, not contributing to improve the results in Traceability Links Recovery or Feature Location.

5 Requirements, bugs, and features can all be described through NL, but are of different nature. Different fitness configurations guide the Evolutionary Algorithm better, depending on the task (Traceability Links Recovery, Bug Localization, Feature Location) that is being carried out: Configuration 1 (Similitude) for Traceability Links Recovery, Configuration 4 (Similitude + Understandability + Timing) for Bug Localization, and Configuration 2 (Similitude + Understandability) for Feature Location.

The results of evaluating our approach show that Traceability Link Recovery achieves the worst results. We detected that this happens because when requirements are written, part of the domain knowledge related to the requirements is assumed to be known by all the domain experts, so it is not formalized. For example, given the requirement: *At all stations, the doors are automatically opened,* the engineers understand that the doors have to be opened in all the stations without being requested by a passenger.

However, this requirement embodies tacit knowledge that is obvious to the domain engineers: *The train has doors on both sides, but only the doors on the side of the platform will be opened while the doors on the side of the tracks will remain closed,* and *all the doors of one side will be opened, except the driver's door in the cabin.*

Tacit knowledge is not reflected in the text of the requirements, since it is shared between the engineers who write and read the requirements. As a result, the models are built through both the text of the requirements, and the tacit knowledge of the engineers, leading to models that contain elements built according to the text of the requirements, and elements built through tacit knowledge.

However, since part of the knowledge is not reflected in the text of the requirement, the similitude objective is negatively influenced. The similitude objective establishes the similarity between the query and the model fragment according to the co-occurrences of terms between both. Configuration 1 (similitude objective only) achieves worse results for Traceability Link Recovery than for Feature Location. Feature descriptions are less vulnerable to the tacit knowledge issue since they are written in a different style, in a different moment of the software life cycle, and with a different goal in mind. Requirements play a key role in the contracts between our industrial partner and their clients, but feature descriptions are for internal use only.

Model understandability does not pay off in the particular case of Traceability Link Recovery. Configurations 2 and 4 (which include the understandability objective) achieve worse results than Configuration 1 (similitude objective only). Model understandability favors model fragments that involve a lower number of model elements. In the face of (1) a model fragment (that includes model elements related to the tacit knowledge), and (2) a model fragment that is a subset of the former (without the model elements related to the tacit knowledge), the first model fragment not only does not achieve a better result for the similitude objective, but it is also penalized by the understandability objective because of its higher model elements count.

Also, our results confirm the relevance of the Defect Principle (Zimmermann et al. 2004) in model fragment retrieval since the configurations that include Model Timing (Configuration 3 and 4) obtained the best results in Bug Location. This is because the majority of bugs (about 90%) provided by our industrial partner are related to recent modifications. In contrast, Model Timing negatively influenced the results in Traceability Links Recovery and Feature Location. Given either a requirement or a feature description, it is not safe to assume than in most of the cases it is related to a model fragment modified recently.

Vocabulary mismatch is a phenomena that occurs when when distinct words are used to refer to the same concept in both query and models. This happens most when the engineer in charge of defining the query (requirement, feature description, or bug description) has not been involved in the construction of the model, and when different engineers are in charge of working with the queries and the models.

Even though we use Natural Language Processing (NLP) to unify the language of the terms shared by queries and models, vocabulary mismatch remains an issue that must be taken into account: the in-house terms are often not recognized as eligible synonyms, and are therefore excluded from NLP, leading to vocabulary mismatch. For example, the terms *PLC* and *system* may be recognized as synonyms, but the terms *PLC* and *COSMOS*[3] are definitely not known to be synonyms, because *COSMOS* is an in-house term that is used exclusively by our industrial partner to refer to the term *PLC*. To minimize the vocabulary mismatch issue, NLP should be extended in order to include a list of in-house synonyms.

Finally, our approach takes as input a query to provide a ranking of solutions that the engineer can inspect instead of having to look for solutions manually. This helps engineers since they do not have to inspect large and complex models manually each time that a software maintenance activity needs to be carried out. The engineers can also consider the solutions of the ranking as a starting point from where solutions can be manually refined.

Furthermore, after inspecting the solutions, the user may refine the query and iterate the process to obtain different solutions. Our findings are encouraging and indicate that we should further research this field.

4.6 Threats to validity

We follow the guidelines suggested by De Oliveira et al. (Oliveira Barros and Neto 2011) to identify the threats to the validity of our work.

Conclusion validity threats: The first threat of this type is not accounting for random variation. To address this threat, we considered 30 independent runs for each query and configuration. The second threat is the lack of a formal hypothesis and statistical tests. In this paper we employed standard statistical analysis following accepted guidelines (Arcuri and Fraser 2013) to avoid this threat. The third threat is the lack of a good descriptive analysis. In this work, we have used the recall, precision and F-measure measurements to analyze the confusion matrix obtained; however, other measurements could be applied. Some works argument that the use of the Vargha and Delaney $\hat{A}_{12}$ measurement can be miss-representative (Arcuri and Fraser 2013) and that data should be pre-transformed before applying it. We did not find any use cases for data pre-transformation that applied to our case study.

Internal validity threats: The first identified threat of this type is the poor parameter settings threat. In this paper we used standard values for the algorithms. As suggested by Arcuri and Fraser (Arcuri and Fraser 2013), default values are good enough to measure the performance of location techniques. These values have been tested in similar algorithms for Feature Location (Lopez-Herrejon et al. 2015). In addition, the tuning of the 'k' value in the application of SVD can affect the results of LSI, and should be further studied (Thomas et al. 2013; Borg, Runeson, and Ardö 2014). Nevertheless, we plan to evaluate all the parameters of our algorithm in a future work. The second threat is the lack of real problem instances. The evaluation of this paper was applied to an industrial case study.

Construct validity threats: The identified threat is the lack of assessing the validity of cost measures threat. To address this threat we performed a fair comparison among the configurations by allocating a fixed amount of wall clock time for each run of the algorithm in order to set the same amount of time to traverse the search space.

External validity threats: In order to mitigate the lack of a clear object selection strategy, our approach uses an industrial case study, which instances are collected from real world problems.

Moreover, our approach has been designed to be generic and applicable not only to the domain of our industrial partner but also to other different domains: the fitness function can be applied to any model conforming to MOF, and the text elements associated to the models are extracted automatically by the approach using the reflective methods provided by the Eclipse Modeling Framework. The requisites to apply our approach are that the set of models conform to MOF, and the query is provided in NL. However, our approach should be applied to other domains before assuring its generalization.

4.7   Related Work

Works related to this one comprehend Traceability Links Recovery, Bug Localization, and Feature Location. Through this section, some of these related works are analyzed and compared with ours.

4.7.1   Traceability Links Recovery

There are several approaches to Traceability Links Recovery, being NLP and LSI the most common. The role of NLP in requirements engineering is vital to the Software Engineering community (Ryan 1993). NLP has been applied to tackle Traceability Links Recovery at several levels of abstraction and specific problems and tasks in works like (Sultanov and Jane Huffman Hayes 2010; Senthil Karthikeyan Sundaram et al. 2010) or (Duan and Cleland-Huang 2007). In (Falessi, Cantone, and Canfora 2013), NLP is used to identify equivalence between requirements, and a series of performance evaluation principles to do so are defined.

The authors conclude that the performance of NLP is determined by the properties of the studied dataset. They measure the properties as a factor to adjust NLP, and apply their principles to an industrial case study. The work presented in (Arora et al. 2015) uses NLP to study how changes in requirements impact other requirements. The authors analyze Traceability Links Recovery between requirements, and use NLP to determine how changes in requirements must propagate. The work presented in (J. H. Hayes, S. K. Sundaram, and Dekhtyar 2006) uses LSI and analyst feedback to trace code to requirements. Finally, the authors of (Eder et al. 2015) consider the possible configurations of LSI when using the technique for Traceability Links Recovery between requirements and test cases, and state that LSI configurations depend on the datasets. They look forward to automatically determining said configuration.

Our work differs from (Ryan 1993; Sultanov and Jane Huffman Hayes 2010; Senthil Karthikeyan Sundaram et al. 2010; Duan and Cleland-Huang 2007), since we do not use NLP as a means of Traceability Links Recovery analysis. We do not evaluate its performance nor the tweaking of NLP as (Falessi, Cantone, and Canfora 2013) does. Instead, we use NLP to unify the input for LSI. In addition, our work also differs from (Arora et al. 2015), since we do not tackle changes in requirements nor Traceability Links Recovery between requirements, but rather study Traceability Links Recovery between requirements and a set of evolving model fragments. Moreover, our work also differs from (J. H. Hayes, S. K. Sundaram, and Dekhtyar 2006) since we do not use feedback from humans in the tracing process and we target models instead of code. In contrast with (Eder et al. 2015), we do not tackle LSI configurations or their impact on Traceability Links Recovery, but rather analyze how different fitness objectives configurations affect the Evolutionary Algorithm when recovering traceability links.

4.7.2 Bug Localization

In recent years, many Bug Localization approaches have been proposed. Lukins et al. (Lukins, Kraft, and Etzkorn 2010) used Latent Dirichlet Allocation (LDA) for predicting the location of a newly reported bug through source code comments and identifiers as information resources. Zhou et al. (Zhou, H. Zhang, and Lo 2012) proposed a revised Vector Space Model (VSM) approach for improving the performance of bug localization, based on the idea that bugs are more likely to appear in larger files, also using the similarity between the text of new bug reports and previously fixed bugs. Thomas et al. (Thomas et al. 2013) evaluated the performance of combinations of IR-based classifiers for bug location in code. Saha et al. (Saha et al. 2013) presented BLUiR, which uses a TF-IDF model baseline. They believe code constructs improve the accuracy of bug localization, so the source code is syntactically parsed into four document fields: class, method, variable, and comment. The summary and the description of a bug report are considered as query fields. Textual similarities are computed for each of the eight document-query pairs, and summarized into a ranking. Kim et al. (D. Kim et al. 2013) propose a one-phase and a two-phase prediction models to recommend files to fix. In the one-phase model, they create features from textual information and meta-data, apply Naïve Bayes to train the model using fixed files as classification labels, and use said model to assign source files to a bug report. In the two-phase model, they apply their one-phase model to classify a new bug report as "predictable" or "deficient", and then make predictions for "predictable" reports. These approaches target code, while our approach targets models to locate the bug realizations. Moreover, these approaches rely on IR techniques only, while ours uses an Evolutionary Algorithm that generates possible solutions. In addition, we tackle how different combinations of objectives affect the results of our approach. Zamani et al (Zamani et al. 2014) proposed an approach to rank source code locations, based on textual similarity with change requests and the use of time meta-data. This approach gives better results than IR techniques, however, it is applied at the source code level. We use a Evolutionary Algorithm to address the location of bugs in models. In our case, the Defect principle is one of the three computed objectives, activated depending on the configuration.

4.7.3 Feature Location

Approaches related to Feature Location comprehend feature and requirement location techniques. Typechef (Kästner et al. 2011) provides an infrastructure to locate code associated to a given feature by analyzing #ifdef directives. Trace analysis (Eisenberg and Volder 2005) is a technique that indicates the executed code at run-time. Some approaches related to feature location use LSI to extract code associated to a feature (Poshyvanyk et al. 2007; D. Liu et al. 2007). These techniques have been generally applied to search code. In contrast, our approach searches for model fragments.

Feature location approaches in product families (Xue, Xing, and Jarzabek 2012) center their efforts in finding the code that implements a feature between different products through FCA (Ganter and R. Wille 2012) and LSI. In our approach, we are instead interested in locating the most relevant model fragments for a feature. Other works (She et al. 2011) focus on applying reverse engineering to source code to obtain the variability model. In (Czarnecki and Wasowski 2007) the authors use propositional logic to describe the dependencies between features. In (Nadi et al. 2014) the authors combine Typechef and propositional logic to extract conditions among features. These works engage the variability of products, but do tackle the most relevant model fragments for the development of features.

In (Lapeña, Ballarín, and Cetina 2016), Lapeña et al. use POS Tagging along with an adapted two-step LSI to obtain rankings of methods for the requirements of a new product in a product family. In the presented work, we use a Multiple Objective Evolutionary Algorithm (MOEA) to find model fragments that can be used to implement a particular feature, and analyze how distinct fitness objective configurations affect the results instead.

Some works (D. Wille, Sönke Holthusen, et al. 2013b; Sönke Holthusen et al. 2014b; X. Zhang, Øystein Haugen, and Møller-Pedersen 2011; X. Zhang, Øystein Haugen, and Møller-Pedersen 2012; Jabier Martinez et al. 2015b) focus on the location of features over models by comparing the models with each other to formalize the variability among them.

The presented work differs from these works in that the aim is not to formalize the variability, but to locate model fragments relevant to the provided feature descriptions.

Font et al. (Font et al. 2016a) use a Single Objective Evolutionary Algorithm (SOEA) to locate features among a family of models. Their approach is refined in (Font et al. 2016b), where the authors use a SOEA to find sets of suitable feature realizations. The authors cluster model fragments based on their common attributes through FCA, and then LSI ranks the candidates based on the similarity with the feature description. The presented approach differs from (Font et al. 2016a) and (Font et al. 2016b) by leveraging a MOEA, with a fitness function that combines three fitness objectives to determine the fitness scores of the evolving model fragments.

In (Font et al. 2017), Font et al. performed a comparison between five different SOEAs (Evolutionary Algorithm, Random Search, Steepest Ascent Hill Climbing with Replacement, Iterated Local Search with Random Restarts, and Hybrid between Evolutionary and Hill-Climbing) for feature location in models, showing that the best results where achieved by a hybrid between an evolutionary algorithm and a hill climbing. Cetina et al. (Cetina et al. 2017) explored a new direction: taking advantage of already long-living software systems (designed with sustainability in mind) to address the challenge of feature location. Specifically, they used commonality and modifications fitness though model retrospectives in order to promote model fragments that suffered less modifications throughout time. Through this work, we analyze the impact that different configurations of objectives (four combinations of similitude, understandability and timing) have over the results depending on the maintenance task that is performed, which is something that (Font et al. 2016a; Font et al. 2016b; Font et al. 2017; Cetina et al. 2017) do not tackle.

4.8   Concluding Remarks

Traceability Links Recovery, Bug Localization, and Feature Location are amongst the most common tasks in the Software Engineering field. However, their application to conceptual models has not received enough attention yet. We propose an approach, named Fragment Retrieval on Models (*FROM*), that uses a Multi-Objective Evolutionary Algorithm to retrieve the most relevant model fragments for different types of queries (NL requirements for Traceability Links Recovery, bug descriptions for Bug Localization, and feature descriptions for Feature Location). Our approach is guided by four configurations that combine three different fitness objectives: Model Similitude, Model Understandability, and Model Timing. Through this work, we analyze the impact of each configuration on the results of the Evolutionary Algorithm for Traceability Links Recovery, Bug Localization, and Feature Location.

Our results show new findings that are relevant for general fragment retrieval approaches since none of the four configurations achieve the best results for all the types of NL queries provided as input. Requirements, bugs and features can be described using NL but depending on the task that is being carried out (Traceability Links Recovery, Bug Localization, Feature Location) different fitness configurations are better. For example, model fragment similitude obtains the best results for Traceability Links Recovery but it is not powerful enough to obtain the best results in Bug Localization, in which model timing is useful to improve the results.

In future iterations of our work, we will perform parameter tuning of the evolutionary algorithm and the dimensions 'k' value of LSI. We also plan to evaluate machine learning techniques, such as the ones of the learning to Rank family (T.-Y. Liu et al. 2009), as fitness objectives that guide the retrieval of model fragments for model maintenance tasks.

Appendix A: Algorithms

Algorithm 1 Random Fragment Generation

1: $E \leftarrow randomElement(model)$
2: $F \leftarrow newFragment(E)$
3: $N \leftarrow neighbor(E)$
4: $random \leftarrow randomInteger < modelSize$
5: $iterator \leftarrow 0$
6: **while** $iterator < random$ **do**
7: $\quad P \leftarrow E$
8: $\quad E \leftarrow N$
9: $\quad F \leftarrow add(E)$
10: $\quad N \leftarrow neighbor(E) \neq P$
11: $\quad$ **if** $N = \phi$ **then**
12: $\quad\quad$ **exit while**
13: $\quad$ **end if**
14: **end while**
15: **return** $fragment$

Algorithm 2 Crossover Operation

1: $M \leftarrow firstParent$
2: $N \leftarrow secondParent$
3: $F \leftarrow fragment(firstParent)$
4: **if** $F \in N$ **then**
5: $\quad I \leftarrow individual(F, N)$
6: $\quad$ **return** I
7: **else**
8: $\quad I \leftarrow individual(F, M)$
9: $\quad$ **return** I
10: **end if**

Algorithm 3 Mutation Operation

1: $O \leftarrow operation$
2: $I \leftarrow individual$
3: **if** $operation = addition$ **then**
4:     $E \leftarrow additionCandidateElement(I)$
5:     $N \leftarrow neighbor(E)$
6:     $I \leftarrow add(N)$
7: **else**
8:     $E \leftarrow removalCandidateElement(I)$
9:     $I \leftarrow remove(E)$
10: **end if**
11: **return** I

Appendix B: Metrics to measure the size of a model fragment

U1 Counting the number of elements in a model: To do this, (Störrle 2014) uses labels, shapes, and lines. Shapes refer to the visual elements of the models, lines refer to connectors, and labels refer to descriptive independent text. This metric neglects diagram differences, implying that all elements contribute the same amount of complexity and information to the diagram.

U2 Weight factors per model element: In (Störrle 2014), the author uses the findings of (Koffka 2013) to classify the elements in the models into three complexity levels, assign weights accordingly, and computing the diagram size as the weighed number of elements. This metric does not take in account the inherent differences between diagrams.

U3 Weight factors per model element per diagram type: The author of (Störrle 2014) computes the information content of diagram elements (e) as the binary logarithm of the set of elements (E) a modeler may choose from: $weight(e) = \log_2(|E|)$.

Chapter 5

Exploring New Directions in Traceability Link Recovery in Models: the Process Models Case

Traceability Links Recovery (TLR) has been a topic of interest for many years. However, TLR in Process Models has not received enough attention yet. Through this work, we study TLR between Natural Language Requirements and Process Models through three different approaches: a Models specific baseline, and two techniques based on Latent Semantic Indexing, used successfully over code. We adapted said code techniques to work for Process Models, and propose them as novel techniques for TLR in Models. The three approaches were evaluated by applying them to an academia set of Process Models, and to a set of Process Models from a real-world industrial case study. Results show that our techniques retrieve better results that the baseline Models technique in both case studies. We also studied why this is the case, and identified Process Models particularities that could potentially lead to improvement opportunities.

5.1 Introduction

Traceability Link Recovery (TLR) has been a subject of investigation for many years within the software engineering community (Gotel and Finkelstein 1994; Spanoudakis and Zisman 2005). Research has shown that affordable Traceability can be critical to the success of a project (Watkins and Neal 1994), and leads to increased maintainability and reliability of software systems by making it possible to verify and trace non-reliable parts (Ghazarian 2010). Specifically, more complete Traceability decreases the expected defect rate in developed software (Rempel and Mäder 2017).

In recent years, TLR has been attracting more attention, becoming a subject of both fundamental and applied research (Parizi, Lee, and Dabbagh 2014). However, most of the works focus on code (Rubin and Chechik 2013), and the application of Traceability Links Recovery techniques to Process Models is a topic that has not received enough attention yet.

Through this work, we study TLR between Natural Language Requirements and Process Models through three different approaches. Given a query Requirement and a Process Model, the three techniques use different means to extract a Model Fragment from the Model, being said Model Fragment relevant to the implementation of the query Requirement. The first technique is a Linguistic technique based on Parts-of-Speech (POS) Tagging and Traceability rules (Spanoudakis, Zisman, et al. 2004). The technique was designed specifically for TLR in Models, and is used as a baseline against which the proposed techniques are compared. The other two techniques (named 'Aggregation' and 'Mutation Search') are based on Latent Semantic Indexing and Singular Value Decomposition, a well-spread Information Retrieval technique that has been applied previously to TLR in code, obtaining good results in the process (Rubin and Chechik 2013). None of the two LSI-based techniques have been applied to extract TLR between Requirements and Process Models previously. Therefore, we adapted them to work for Process Models and propose them as novel techniques in the field.

The three approaches were evaluated through the Camunda BPMN for Research case study[1], as well as through a real-world industrial case study, provided by our industrial partner, CAF[2] (Construcciones y Auxiliar de Ferrocarriles), a worldwide provider of railway solutions.

Results show that the Mutation Search technique achieves the best results for all the measured performance indicators in both case studies, providing a mean precision value of 63%, a mean recall value of 77%, a combined F-measure of 68%, and an MCC value of 0.60 for the Camunda BPMN for Research case study, and a mean precision value of 79%, a mean recall value of 72%, a combined F-measure of 74%, and an MCC value of 0.69 for the CAF case study. In contrast, the Linguistic baseline and the Aggregation technique present worse results in these same measurements in both case studies.

The overall findings of our paper suggest that adapting techniques that have provided good results in code is beneficial for TLR between Requirements and Process Models, since their results outperform those of a technique created specifically with Models in mind. Moreover, studied why this is the case, and identified Process Models particularities that could potentially lead to improvement opportunities.

The rest of the paper is structured as follows: Section 5.2 describes our Approach, that is, our proposed techniques and how to apply them to TLR between Requirements and Process Model fragments. Section 5.3 details the baseline technique and the designed Evaluation. Section 5.4 presents the obtained results. Section 5.5 discusses the outcomes of the paper. Section 5.6 presents the Threats to Validity of our work. Section 5.7 reviews the works related to this one. Finally, Section 5.8 concludes the paper.

5.2 Approach

Through the following paragraphs, we give an introduction on Latent Semantic Indexing, the technique upon which we base the two novel techniques proposed for TLR between Requirements and Process Models. Afterwards, we describe said techniques, providing insight on their steps, application, and outcomes.

5.2.1 Latent Semantic Indexing

Latent Semantic Indexing (LSI) (Landauer, Foltz, and Laham 1998) is an automatic mathematical/statistical technique that analyzes relationships between *queries* and *documents* (bodies of text). LSI has been successfully used to retrieve Traceability Links between different kinds of software artifacts in different contexts, specially among Requirements and code (Rubin and Chechik 2013). This is due to the fact that code often encodes domain knowledge in the form of domain terms, which are also encoded in the Requirements, hence causing LSI to detect similitude between both.

So far, the technique has not been transported to Process Models. We propose two techniques that use LSI for TLR between Requirements and Process Models. In particular, both techniques use LSI to produce a Model Fragment from the Process Model that serves as a candidate for realizing the Requirement. The following sections give more details on the process.

5.2.2 Aggregation

The first of the two proposed techniques receives a *query* Requirement and a Process Model as input, and generates a ranking of Model Elements through LSI. From the ranking, a Model Fragment is generated. To that extent, the Process Model is firstly split into Model Elements, represented through the text they contain, which is extracted and used as input for LSI.

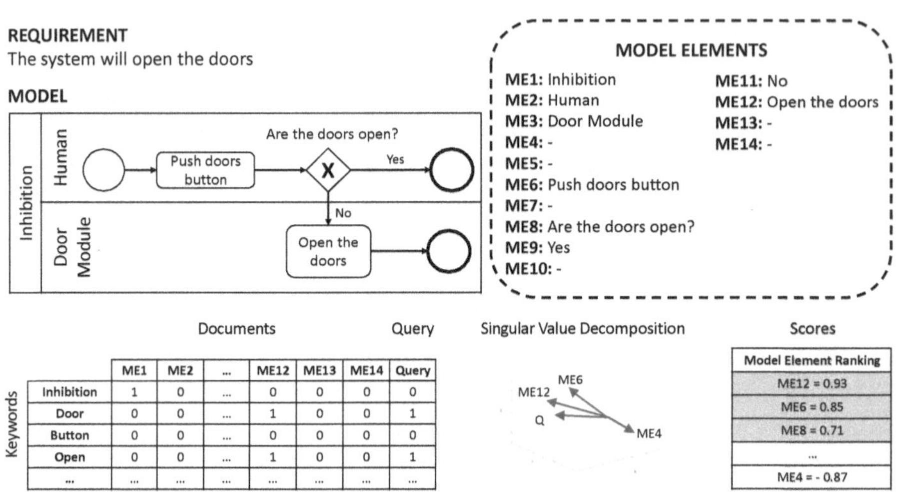

Keywords		ME1	ME2	...	ME12	ME13	ME14	Query
	Inhibition	1	0	...	0	0	0	0
	Door	0	0	...	1	0	0	1
	Button	0	0	...	0	0	0	0
	Open	0	0	...	1	0	0	1
	...	...	...	...	...	...	...	...

Figure 5.1: Aggregation Technique Example

The top part of Fig. 5.1 shows this process, having the example input Process Model on the left, and the resulting Model Elements on the right, including: (1) lanes 'Inhibition', 'Human', and 'PLC' (ME1, ME2, ME3); (2) the start and end events (ME4, ME10, ME14); (3) the exclusive gateway 'Are the doors open?' (ME8); (4) the 'Push the doors button' and 'Open the doors' tasks (ME6, ME12); and (5) the sequence flows of the diagram (ME5, ME7, ME9, ME11, ME13).

The text of the Requirement and the Model Elements is then treated through Natural Language Processing techniques. To that extent, general phrase styling techniques, Parts-Of-Speech Tagging (Hulth n.d.), and Lemmatizing (Plisson, Lavrac, Mladenic, et al. n.d.) are applied.

Finally, the Requirement and the Model Elements are fed into LSI, which ranks the Model Elements according to their similitude to the Requirement. The bottom left part of Fig. 5.1 shows an example *term-by-document co-occurrence matrix*, with values associated to our running example. In the following paragraph, an overview of the elements of the matrix is provided.

Each row in the matrix (*term*) stands for each of the words that appear in the processed text of the Requirement and the Model Elements. In Fig. 5.1, it is possible to notice a subset of said words such as 'Door' or 'Button' as the *terms* of each row. Each column in the matrix (*document*) stands for each of the Model Elements extracted from the input Process Model. In Fig. 5.1, it is possible to notice identifiers in the columns such as 'ME3' or 'ME12', which stand for the *documents* of those particular Model Elements (namely, the processed text of 'ME3' and 'ME12'). The final column (*query*), stands for the processed input Requirement. Each cell in the matrix contains the frequency of each *term* in each *document*. For instance, in Fig. 5.1, the *term* 'Door' appears once in the 'ME12' *document* and once in the *query*.

Vector representations of the *documents* and the *query* are obtained by normalizing and decomposing the *term-by-document co-occurrence matrix* using a matrix factorization technique called *Singular Value Decomposition* (SVD) (Landauer, Foltz, and Laham 1998). SVD is a form of factor analysis, or more properly the mathematical generalization of which factor analysis is a special case. In SVD, a rectangular matrix is decomposed into the product of three other matrices. One component matrix describes the original row entities as vectors of derived orthogonal factor values, another describes the original column entities in the same way, and the third is a diagonal matrix containing scaling values such that when the three components are matrix-multiplied, the original matrix is reconstructed.

In Fig. 5.1, a three-dimensional graph of the SVD is provided, on which it is possible to notice the vectorial representations of some of the columns. For legibility reasons, only a small set of the columns is represented. To measure the similarity degree between vectors, the cosine between the *query* vector and the *documents* vectors is calculated. Cosine values closer to one denote a high degree of similarity, and cosine values closer to minus one denote a low degree of similarity. Similarity increases as vectors point in the same general direction (as more *terms* are shared between *documents*). Through this measurement, the Model Elements are ordered according to their similarity degree to the Requirement.

The relevancy ranking (which can be seen in Fig. 5.1) is produced according to the calculated similarity values. In this example, LSI retrieves 'ME12', 'ME6', and 'ME8' in the first, second, and third position of the relevancy ranking due to their *query-documents* cosines being '0.9343', '0.8524' and '0.7112', implying high similarity between the Model Elements and the Requirement. On the opposite, the 'ME4' Model Element is returned in a latter position of the ranking due to its *query-document* cosine being '-0.8736', implying a low similarity degree.

From the ranking, of all the Model Elements, those that have a similarity measure greater than x must be taken into account. The heuristic that we adopted, and that is used in other works, is $x = 0.7$ (Marcus et al. 2004; Salman, Seriai, and Dony 2014). This value corresponds to a 45° angle between the corresponding vectors. Nevertheless, the selection of this threshold is an issue still under study, and its proper parametrization has not been tackled in Process Models yet.

Following this principle, the Model Elements with a similarity measure equal or superior to $x = 0.7$ are taken to conform a Model Fragment, candidate for realizing the Requirement. Through the example provided in Fig. 5.1, 'ME12', 'ME6' and 'ME8' are the Model Elements that conform the Model Fragment for the Requirement, due to their cosine values being superior to the 0.7 threshold. The Model Elements below the threshold, except for 'ME4', are not shown in the ranking for space and understandability reasons. The Model Fragment generated in this manner is the final output of the Aggregation technique.

5.2.3 *Mutation Search*

The second of the two proposed techniques receives a *query* Requirement and a Process Model as input, generates a population of Model Fragments, and ranks said Model Fragments through LSI. From the ranking, the first Model Fragment is taken as the proposed solution. In order to generate the Model Fragments population, algorithm 4 is followed. In the algorithm, an empty population and a seed Fragment (chosen randomly from the input Process Model) are created.

Then, until the algorithm mets a stop condition (for instance, a certain number of iterations), the Fragment is mutated and each new mutation is added to the population, avoiding the addition of repeated Fragments.

In the algorithm, a mutation in a Fragment can be caused by: (1) adding one new event, gateway, or task that is connected to an already present event, gateway, or task (the flow that causes the connection is also added to the Fragment), (2) removing an Element with only one connection (and the flow that causes said connection), or (3) adding or removing a lane from the Fragment. The performed mutation is chosen randomly on each iteration.

Algorithm 4 Mutation Search Algorithm

1: $P \leftarrow []$ ▷ Initialize the population
2: $F \leftarrow randomFragment(inputModel)$ ▷ Create an initial seed Fragment
3: **while** $!(StopCondition)$ **do**   ▷ While the stop condition is not met
4:    $F \leftarrow mutateFragment(F)$ ▷ Mutate the Fragment
5:    **if** $!(F \in P)$ **then**   ▷ If the new Fragment is not in the population
6:     $P \leftarrow P + F$ ▷ Add the new mutation to the population
7:    **end if**
8: **end while**
9: **return** P ▷ Return the population

The top part of Fig. 5.2 shows this process, having the example input Process Model on the left, and some example Model Fragments on the right, generated through the usage of the algorithm. The generated Model Fragments are represented through the text contained in all their elements. The text of both the input Requirement and the generated Model Fragments is then processed through general phrase styling techniques, Parts-Of-Speech Tagging, and Lemmatizing.

Finally, the Requirement and the Model Fragments are fed into LSI, which ranks the Model Fragments according to their similitude to the Requirement. The bottom left part of Fig. 5.2 shows an example *term-by-document co-occurrence matrix*, with values associated to our running example.

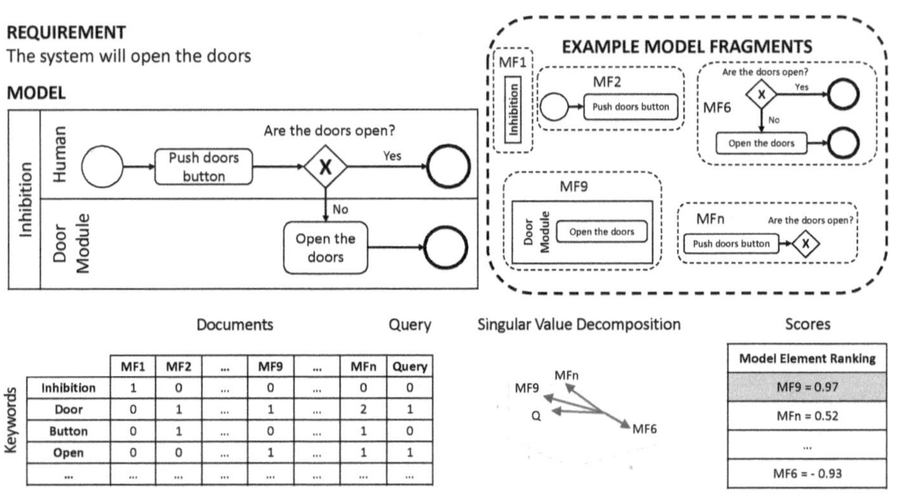

Keywords	MF1	MF2	...	MF9	...	MFn	Query
Inhibition	1	0	...	0	...	0	0
Door	0	1	...	1	...	2	1
Button	0	1	...	0	...	1	0
Open	0	0	...	1	...	1	1
...	...	...	...	...	...	...	...

Figure 5.2: Mutation Search Technique Example

The technique works exactly as it does in the Aggregation technique, except that each column in the matrix (*document*) stands for each of the Model Fragments (MF1 to MFn) generated through the algorithm instead of standing for a single Model Element.

Vector representations of the *documents* and the *query* are obtained by normalizing and decomposing the *term-by-document co-occurrence matrix* using SVD, and the vectorial similarity degrees are calculated through the cosines. The relevancy ranking on Fig. 5.2 is produced according to the calculated similarity degrees. In this example, LSI retrieves 'MF9' in the first position of the relevancy ranking due to its *query-documents* cosine being '0.9791'. On the opposite, the 'MF6' Model Fragment is returned in the last position of the ranking due to its *query-document* cosine being '-0.9384'.

From the ranking, the first Model Fragment is considered as the candidate solution for the Requirement, and consequently taken as the final output of the Mutation Search technique.

5.3 Evaluation

Through the following paragraphs, we introduce the experimental setup and the case studies used to evaluate the baseline and our two proposed approaches, present the oracles used in the evaluation, and detail the design and implementation of said evaluation.

5.3.1 Experimental Setup

The goal of our work is to perform TLR between Requirements and Process Models through the two proposed techniques, and to compare the results obtained by said techniques against those of a Models specific baseline. Fig. 5.3 shows an overview of the process that was followed to evaluate the Linguistic baseline and our two proposed techniques. The top part shows the inputs, which are extracted from the documentation provided in the case studies: Requirements, Process Models, and approved Traceability between Requirements and Process Models. Each case study comprises a set of Requirements, a Process Model, and an Approved Requirements to Model Fragments Traceability document, which conforms the oracle of our evaluation.

For each case study, the Linguistic baseline and the Aggregation technique take the mentioned inputs, and generate a single Model Fragment for each Requirement. The generated Model Fragments are compared with the oracle Model Fragment. The Mutation Search technique generates a ranking of Model Fragments per Requirement instead. Since the rankings are ordered from best to worst Traceability, the first Model Fragment in each ranking is picked for comparison against its corresponding oracle. Once the comparisons are performed, a confusion matrix is calculated for the baseline and for each technique separately.

A confusion matrix is a table that is often used to describe the performance of a classification Model (in this case the Linguistic baseline and both of our techniques) on a set of test data (the solutions) for which the true values are known (from the oracle). In our case, each solution outputted by the three techniques is a Model Fragment composed of a subset of the Model Elements that are part of the Process Model.

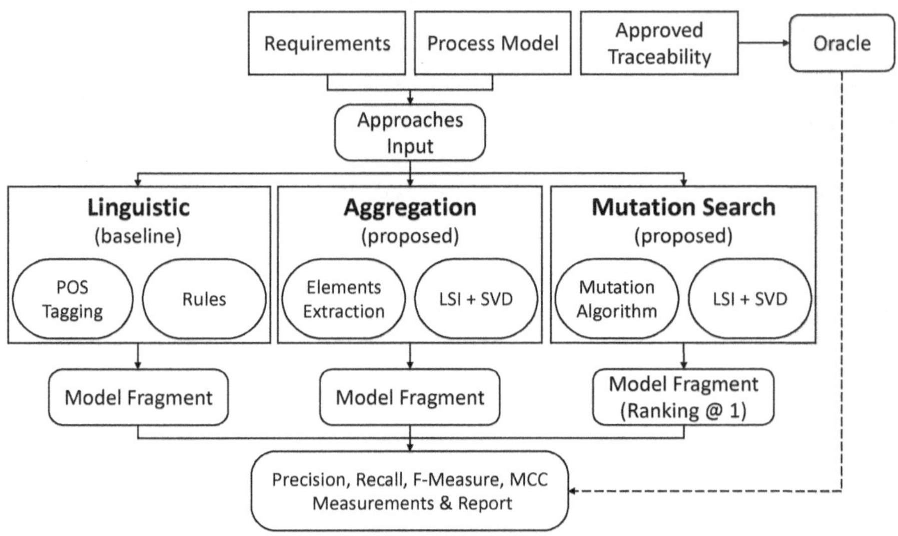

Figure 5.3: Experimental Setup

Since the granularity is at the level of Model Elements, the presence or absence of each Model Element is considered as a classification. The confusion matrix distinguishes between the predicted values and the real values, classifying them into four categories: (1) True Positive (TP), values that are predicted as true (in the solution), and are true in the real scenario (the oracle); (2) False Positive (FP), values that are predicted as true (in the solution), but are false in the real scenario (the oracle); (3) True Negative (TN), values that are predicted as false (in the solution), and are false in the real scenario (the oracle); and (4) False Negative (FN), values that are predicted as false (in the solution), but are true in the real scenario (the oracle).

Then, some performance measurements are derived from the values in the confusion matrix. In particular, a report including four performance measurements (Recall, Precision, F-measure, and Matthews Correlation Coefficient) is created for the case studies, for each of the three techniques.

Recall measures the number of elements of the solution that are correctly retrieved by the proposed solution. Precision measures the number of elements from the solution that are correct according to the ground truth. F-measure corresponds to the harmonic mean of Precision and Recall (Salton and McGill 1986).

However, none of these previous measures correctly handle negative examples (TN). The **MCC** is a correlation coefficient between the observed and predicted binary classifications that takes into account all the observed values (TP, TN, FP, FN), and is defined as follows:

$$MCC = \frac{TP \cdot TN - FP \cdot FN}{\sqrt{(TP + FP)(TP + FN)(TN + FP)(TN + FN)}}$$

Recall values can range between 0% (which means that no single model element from the realization of the requirement obtained from the oracle is present in the model fragment of the solution) to 100% (which means that all the model elements from the oracle are present in the solution). Precision values can range between 0% (which means that no single model element from the solution is the oracle) to 100% (which means that all the model elements from the solution are present in the oracle). A value of 100% precision and 100% recall implies that both the solution and the requirement realization from the oracle are the same. MCC values can range between -1 (which means that there is no correlation between the prediction and the solution) to 1 (which means that the prediction is perfect). Moreover, a MCC value of 0 corresponds to a random prediction.

5.3.2 Linguistic Rule-Based Baseline

Spanoudakis et al. (Spanoudakis, Zisman, et al. 2004) present a linguistic rule-based approach to support the automatic generation of Traceability Links between Natural Language Requirements and Models.

Specifically, the Traceability Links are generated following two stages: (1) a Parts-of-Speech (POS) tagging technique (Leech, Garside, and Bryant 1994) is applied on the Requirements that are defined using Natural Language, and (2) the Traceability Links between the Requirements and the Models are generated through a set of *Requirement-to-object-Model* (RTOM) rules.

The RTOM rules are specified by investigating grammatical patterns in Requirements. These rules are specified as sequences of terms, and define relations between Requirements and Model Elements. For instance, a rule may attempt to match a *verb-article-noun* pattern that appears in a Requirement with the text that appears in a Model Element. The rules are atomic: the matching succeeds if the Model Element contains the same words in the same pattern.

In (Spanoudakis, Zisman, et al. 2004), the authors propose 26 rules, applied to a Requirement and a Model in order to retrieve a set of Model Elements from the Model that are related to the Requirement. These Model Elements compose the Model Fragment as a result. We worked with a set of rules adapted to work over Process Models.

5.3.3 Case Study

In order to perform the evaluation of the three approaches, we rely on two different case studies: (1) the Camunda BPMN for Research academic repository, and (2) a set of Process Models provided by CAF, our industrial partner.

Camunda BPMN for Research: The Camunda BPMN for Research case study consists of four Process Modeling exercises. Each exercise contains an associated textual description and the solution Model for the provided description. In order to apply the three approaches to the Camunda case study, a software engineer (with BPMN expertise, and who is not related to the writing of this paper) derived a set of Natural Language Requirements from the problem descriptions. On average, there are around 15 Requirements per problem, with an approximate average of 25 words per requirement. The Models in the case study contain an approximate average of 25 elements per Model.

CAF: For our evaluation, CAF provided us with Natural Language Requirements and Process Models of five railway solutions from Auckland, Bucharest, Cincinnati, Houston, and Kaohsiung. The functionalities are specified through about 100 Natural Language Requirements each, with an approximate average of 50 words per Requirement. Regarding the Process Models, the distinct functionalities are specified through an average 850 total model elements.

5.3.4 Oracle

In order to obtain the performance results of the three approaches, their outcomes must be compared against the correct solutions of the two case studies.

Camunda BPMN for Research: In the case of the Camunda BPMN for Research case study, each exercise has an associated solution Model for the provided description. The same software engineer who derived the Natural Language Requirements from the problem descriptions also generated a set of Model Fragments from the solution Model, mapping each Fragment to a single Requirement. Thus, we were provided with a set of Requirements, the Model Fragments that implement them, and the TLR mapping between both artifacts.

CAF: Regarding our industrial partner, CAF provided us with their existing documentation on Requirements to Process Models Traceability, where each requirement is also mapped to a single Model Fragment.

In both cases, we use the existing Traceability as the oracle for evaluating the outcomes of each of the three approaches. To do so, we compare the Model Fragments generated for each Requirement by the three of them against the oracle Model Fragment (ground truth Model Fragment) for said Requirements.

5.3.5   Implementation details

We have used three libraries to implement the different approaches taken in account through this work: (1) to load and process the Process Models in both case studies, we used the Camunda BPMN Model API (Camunda 2017), (2) to develop the Natural Language Processing operations in our approaches, we have used the OpenNLP Toolkit for the Processing of Natural Language Text (Apache 2016), and (3) to perform the LSI and SVD carried out in the Aggregation and Mutation Search techniques, the Efficient Java Matrix Library (EJML) was used (Abeles n.d.). For the evaluation, we used a Lenovo E330 laptop, with a processor Intel(R) Core(TM) i5-3210M@2.5GHz with 16GB RAM and Windows 10 64-bit.

5.4   Results

Table 5.1 outlines the results of the three studied approaches. Each row shows the Precision, Recall, F-measure, and MCC values obtained through each technique.

The Mutation Search technique achieves the best results for all the performance indicators in both case studies, providing a mean precision value of 63%, a mean recall value of 77%, a combined F-measure of 68%, and an MCC value of 0.60 for the Camunda BPMN for Research case study, and a mean precision value of 79%, a mean recall value of 72%, a combined F-measure of 74%, and an MCC value of 0.69 for the CAF case study. In contrast, both the Linguistic technique and the Aggregation technique present worse results in all the measurements.

The Linguistic technique attains a mean precision value of 40%, a mean recall value of 35%, a combined F-measure of 33%, and an MCC value of 0.25 for the Camunda BPMN for Research case study, and a mean precision value of 35%, a mean recall value of 35%, a combined F-measure of 33%, and an MCC value of 0.25 for the CAF case study.

The Aggregation technique attains a mean precision value of 56%, a mean recall value of 72%, a combined F-measure of 61%, and an MCC value of 0.52 for the Camunda BPMN for Research case study, and a mean precision value of 69%, a mean recall value of 66%, a combined F-measure of 64%, and an MCC value of 0.58 for the CAF case study.

Table 5.1: Mean Values and Standard Deviations for Precision, Recall and F-Measure for the three approaches

	Precision	Recall	F-Measure	MCC
Linguistic - Camunda	40%±25%	35%±22%	33%±13%	0.25±0.19
Linguistic - CAF	35%±28%	35%±10%	30%±7%	0.18±0.13
Aggregation - Camunda	56%±18%	72%±22%	61%±17%	0.52±0.24
Aggregation - CAF	69%±29%	66%±17%	64%±17%	0.58±0.21
Mutation Search - Camunda	63%±21%	77%±22%	68%±19%	0.60±0.24
Mutation Search - CAF	79%±19%	72%±19%	74%±16%	0.69±0.20

5.5   Discussion

The Linguistic technique depends strongly on the language of the Requirements and Models: for a link to be produced between a Requirement a Model Element, exact patterns of words must be atomically matched through the rules. If a single word in a pattern found in a Requirement is different (or missing) in the Model, the rule does not trigger and the link is not produced. On the other hand, in the Aggregation and Mutation Search techniques the atomicity of text patterns is abandoned in favor of the semantic similitude of individual terms. This issue can be illustrated through an example. Consider the Requirement *'The system will open the doors'*, and a Model where the term *'system'* has been swapped for the more technical term *'PLC'*. Due to the vocabulary mismatch, the Linguistic technique would never find the pattern, and thus could never generate the links between Requirement and Model. On the other hand, our techniques would flag the occurrences of the terms *'open'* and *'doors'* in the corresponding Model Elements or Fragments, leading to a potential finding of links.

Moreover, Model Elements with little or no text appear often in Process Models, mainly in the form of flows and sometimes in the form of events. These elements can never be retrieved by the Linguistic technique: since there are no words, there is no pattern that can be matched. They are not retrieved by the Aggregation technique either: they tend to be at the bottom of the ranking produced by LSI since for these elements, all the *term* occurrences are equal to zero and thus, no correlation can be found with the *query* Requirement. However, in the Mutation Search technique, the algorithm does add these Elements to the candidate Fragments. Moreover, the addition of these Elements does not penalize the results technique, since the *term* occurrences are not altered in any way by them. Therefore, the candidate Fragments are more correct and complete, which leads the technique to better Precision and Recall results.

Finally, we also identified certain Process Models particularities that, if leveraged, would improve our Traceability techniques. Some examples of these particularities are: (1) the usage of the term 'if' in a Requirement almost always indicates the presence of an associated gateway in the Process Model, (2) the usage of the terms 'start' or 'end' usually denote events of the same type, (3) questions are often related with gateways in the Models, (4) verbs appear mostly on tasks, or (5) a noun that is often repeated at the start of multiple requirements may be the subject that carries an action (and thus, may appear in the Model as a lane). By studying the patterns of the Process Models language, it could be possible to take in account these particularities in our techniques (by, for instance, weighing the Model Elements accordingly or forcing their appearance), leading them to enhanced Traceability results.

5.6 Threats to Validity

In this section, we use the classification of threats to validity of (Wohlin et al. 2012) to acknowledge the limitations of our approach.

Construct validity: To minimize this risk, our evaluation is performed using four measures: Precision, Recall, F-measure, and MCC. These measures are widely accepted in the software engineering research community.

Internal Validity: The number of requirements and Process Models presented in this work may look small, but they represent a wide scope of different scenarios in an accurate manner.

External Validity: Both Natural Language Descriptions and Business Process Models are frequently leveraged to specify all kinds of different Business Processes. The Camunda Process for Research case study provides different examples from radically different domains. In addition, the real-world CAF Process Models used in our research are a good representative of the railway, automotive, aviation, and general industrial manufacturing domains. Our approach does not rely on the particular conditions of any of those domains. Nevertheless, our results should be replicated with other case studies before assuring their generalization.

Reliability: To reduce this threat, the requirements and Process Models used in our approach were taken from an open-source case study and from an industrial case study. None of the authors of this work was involved in the generation of said data.

5.7 Related Work

Related works focus on the impact and application of Linguistic techniques to TLR problem resolution at several levels of abstraction. Works like (Sultanov and Hayes 2010; Sundaram et al. 2010) or (Duan and Cleland-Huang 2007), among many others, use Linguistic approaches to tackle specific TLR problems and tasks. In (Falessi, Cantone, and Canfora 2013), the authors use Linguistic techniques to identify equivalence between Requirements, also defining and using a series of principles for evaluating their performance when identifying equivalent Requirements. The authors of (Falessi, Cantone, and Canfora 2013) conclude that, in their field, the performance of Linguistic techniques is determined by the properties of the given dataset over which they are performed. They measure the properties as a factor to adjust the Linguistic techniques accordingly, and then apply their principles to an industrial case study.

The work presented in (Arora et al. 2015) uses Linguistic techniques to study how changes in Requirements impact other Requirements in the same specification. Through the pages of their work, the authors analyze TLR between Requirements, and use Linguistic techniques to determine how changes in requirements must propagate.

Our work differs from (Ryan 1993; Sultanov and Hayes 2010; Sundaram et al. 2010; Duan and Cleland-Huang 2007) since our approach is not based or focused on Linguistic techniques as a means of TLR analysis, but we rather propose novel techniques to perform TLR between Requirements and Process Models, using a Linguistic technique only as a baseline against which our work is compared. Moreover, we do not study how Linguistic techniques must be tweaked for specific problems as (Falessi, Cantone, and Canfora 2013) does. In addition, differing from (Arora et al. 2015), we do not tackle changes in Requirements nor TLR between Requirements, but instead focus our work on TLR between Requirements and Process Models.

Finally, other works target the application of LSI to TLR tasks. De Lucia et al. (De Lucia et al. 2004) present a tool based on LSI in the context of an artifact management system. (Eder et al. 2015) takes in consideration the possible configurations of LSI when using the technique for TLR between Requirements artifacts. In their work, the authors state that the configurations of LSI depend on the datasets used, and they look forward to automatically determining an appropriate configuration for LSI for any given dataset. Through our work, we do not study the management of artifacts nor different LSI configurations or how LSI configurations impact the results of TLR, but we rather study TLR between Requirements and Process Models.

5.8 Conclusions

Traceability Links Recovery (TLR) has been a topic of interest for many years, but its study is an issue that has not received enough attention yet in the field of Process Models.

Through this paper, we have studied TLR between Natural Language Requirements and Process Models through three different approaches: a Linguistic approach based on rules, specific from Models (which acts as a baseline for our work), and two techniques (Aggregation and Mutation Search) that we proposed and which we based on Latent Semantic Indexing, a technique that has been used successfully over code. The retrieved TLR results can be utilized by software engineers as a starting point for the development of their solutions.

The three approaches were evaluated by applying them to an academia set of Process Models, and to a set of Process Models from a real-world industrial case study with our industrial partner, CAF, a worldwide manufacturer of railway solutions. Results show that our techniques retrieve better results that the baseline Linguistic technique in both case studies. Through this work, we analyzed why this is the case, and identified some particularities of Process Modeling that could be used in order to improve our techniques in future iterations of our work.

Chapter 6

Traceability Links Recovery in BPMN Models

Traceability Links Recovery has been a topic of interest for many years. However, Traceability Links Recovery in models in general, and BPMN models in particular, has not received enough attention yet. Through my work, I aim to fill this research gap by studying Traceability Links Recovery between requirements and BPMN models. So far, under the tutelage of directors Carlos Cetina and Óscar Pastor, I adapted Traceability Links Recovery code techniques to work over BPMN models. The produced approach was applied to two different case studies, an academic one and an industrial one. The outcomes of the research outperformed the state of the art baseline. Under the light of these novel findings, opportunities for new research unfold.

6.1   Introduction

Traceability Links Recovery (TLR) is defined as the software engineering task that deals with the identification and comprehension of dependencies and relationships between software artifacts. It has been a subject of investigation for many years within the software engineering community Gotel and Finkelstein 1994; Spanoudakis and Zisman 2005. Research has shown that affordable traceability can be critical to the success of a project Watkins and Neal 1994, and leads to increased maintainability and reliability of software systems Ghazarian 2010, also decreasing the expected defect rate in developed software Rempel and Mäder 2017. In recent years, TLR has been attracting more attention Parizi, Lee, and Dabbagh 2014. However, most of the works focus on performing TLR tasks in code artifacts Rubin and Chechik 2013, while TLR in process models is a topic that has not received enough attention yet. Through my work, I aim to fill this research gap by studying TLR between requirements and process models. So far, under the tutelage of directors Carlos Cetina and Óscar Pastor, I adapted TLR code techniques to work over process models (specifically, BPMN models). More precisely, through the work presented in Lapeña et al. 2018, we studied TLR between requirements and process models through three different approaches, two adapted code techniques and a models-specific baseline. Given a query requirement and a process model, the three approaches used different means to extract a fragment from the model, relevant to the implementation of the query requirement.

The three approaches were evaluated through the Camunda BPMN for Research case study[1] and through a real-world industrial case study, provided by our industrial partner, CAF[2] (Construcciones y Auxiliar de Ferrocarriles), a worldwide provider of railway solutions. One of the adapted code techniques achieved the best results for all the measured performance indicators in both case studies, outperforming the other two techniques.

The overall findings of our paper suggested that adapting code techniques that provided good results in code was beneficial for TLR between requirements and BPMN models, since the outcomes outperformed those of a models-specific baseline. Under the light of these findings, a research question arises, unfolding opportunities for novel research: *How can we further improve TLR in BPMN models?*

The rest of the paper is structured as follows: Section 6.2 describes the Approach that obtained the best results and how to apply it to TLR between requirements and BPMN models. Section 6.3 details the baseline technique and the designed Evaluation. Section 6.4 presents the obtained Results. Section 6.5 formulates the Research Question that arises from our ongoing work. Section 6.6 discusses potential Future Work. Section 6.7 mentions the research Methodology in use. Finally, Section 6.8 reviews the works related to this one.

6.2 Approach

This section describes the Mutation Search technique, the technique designed in Lapeña et al. 2018 that obtained the best results for TLR between requirements and BPMN models, providing insight on its steps, application, and outcomes.

6.2.1 Mutation Search

The Mutation Search technique receives one *query* requirement and one BPMN model as input, generates a population of fragments, and ranks said fragments through Latent Semantic Indexing. From the ranking, the first fragment is taken as the proposed solution. In order to generate the fragments population, algorithm 5 is followed. In the algorithm, an empty population and a seed fragment (chosen randomly from the input model) are created. Then, until the algorithm meets a stop condition (for instance, a certain number of iterations), the fragment is mutated and each new mutation is added to the population, avoiding the addition of repeated fragments.

In the algorithm, a mutation in a fragment can be caused by: (1) adding one new event, gateway, or task that is connected to an already present event, gateway, or task, (2) removing an element with only one connection, or (3) adding or removing a lane from the fragment. The performed mutation is chosen randomly on each iteration.

Algorithm 5 Mutation Search Algorithm

1: $P \leftarrow []$ ▷ Initialize the population
2: $F \leftarrow randomFragment(inputModel)$ ▷ Create an initial seed fragment
3: **while** $!(StopCondition)$ **do**   ▷ While the stop condition is not met
4:     $F \leftarrow mutateFragment(F)$ ▷ Mutate the fragment
5:     **if** $!(F \in P)$ **then**   ▷ If the new fragment is not in the population
6:        $P \leftarrow P + F$ ▷ Add the new mutation to the population
7:     **end if**
8: **end while**
9: **return** P ▷ Return the population

The top part of Fig. 6.1 shows this process, having the example input BPMN model on the left, and some example fragments on the right, generated through the usage of the algorithm. The generated fragments are represented through the text contained in all their elements. The text of both the input requirement and the generated fragments is then processed through general phrase styling techniques (lowercasing and tokenization), Parts-Of-Speech Tagging Hulth n.d., and Lemmatizing Plisson, Lavrac, Mladenic, et al. n.d.

Finally, the requirement and the fragments are fed into Latent Semantic Indexing, which ranks the fragments according to their similitude to the requirement. Latent Semantic Indexing (LSI) Landauer, Foltz, and Laham 1998 is an automatic mathematical/statistical technique that analyzes relationships between *queries* and *documents* (bodies of text). LSI has been successfully used to retrieve Traceability Links between different kinds of software artifacts in different contexts Rubin and Chechik 2013.

To that extent, LSI produces a *term-by-document co-ocurrence matrix*. The bottom left part of Fig. 6.1 shows an example *term-by-document co-occurrence matrix*, with values associated to an example.

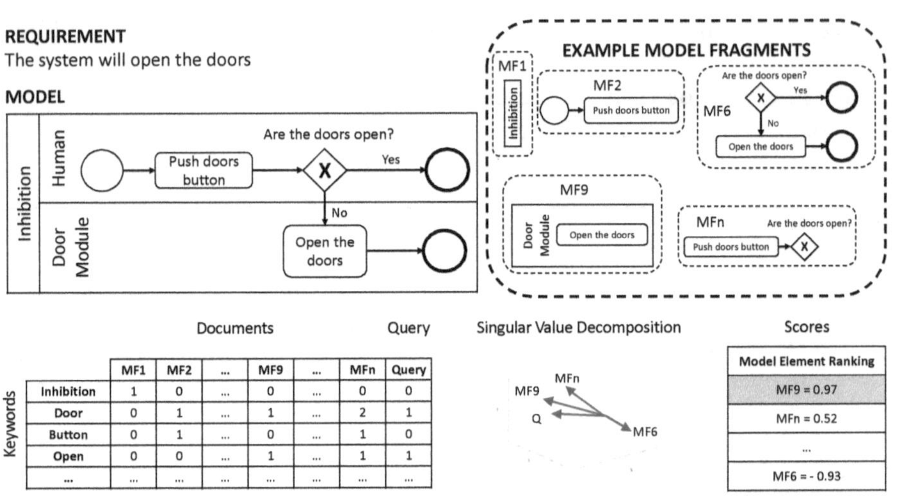

Keywords	MF1	MF2	...	MF9	...	MFn	Query
Inhibition	1	0	...	0	...	0	0
Door	0	1	...	1	...	2	1
Button	0	1	...	0	...	1	0
Open	0	0	...	1	...	1	1
...	...	...	...	...	...	...	...

Figure 6.1: Mutation Search Technique Example

Each row in the matrix (*term*) stands for each of the words that appear in the processed text of the requirement and the model elements. Each column in the matrix (*document*) stands for each of the fragments (MF1 to MFn) generated through the algorithm. The final column (*query*), stands for the processed input requirement. Each cell in the matrix contains the frequency of each *term* in each *document*.

Vector representations of the *documents* and the *query* are obtained by normalizing and decomposing the *term-by-document co-occurrence matrix* using a matrix factorization technique called *Singular Value Decomposition* (SVD) Landauer, Foltz, and Laham 1998. In Fig. 6.1, a three-dimensional graph of the SVD is provided, on which it is possible to notice the vectorial representations of some of the columns. To measure the similarity degree between vectors, the cosine between the *query* vector and the *documents* vectors is calculated. Cosine values closer to one denote a high degree of similarity, and cosine values closer to minus one denote a low degree of similarity.

Through this measurement, the fragments are ordered according to their similarity degree to the requirement, producing the relevancy ranking shown on the bottom right part of Fig. 6.1. From the ranking, the first fragment is considered as the candidate solution for the requirement, and consequently taken as the final output of the Mutation Search technique.

6.3   Evaluation

The following paragraphs introduce the baseline, the experimental setup, the case studies, and the oracles used to evaluate the baseline and Mutation Search. This section also details the design of the evaluation.

6.3.1   Linguistic Rule-Based Baseline

Spanoudakis et al. Spanoudakis, Zisman, et al. 2004 present a linguistic rule-based approach to support the automatic generation of traceability links between natural language requirements and conceptual models. Specifically, the traceability links between the requirements and the conceptual models are generated through a set of *requirement-to-object-model* (RTOM) rules that specify sequences of terms and grammatical patterns. The technique searches for matching patterns in the requirements and the conceptual models, producing a link per each found match. We worked with a set of rules adapted so that the technique works over BPMN models.

6.3.2   Experimental Setup

Through Lapeña et al. 2018, TLR between requirements and BPMN models is performed. The results obtained by Mutation Search are compared against those of a models-specific baseline. An overview evaluation can be seen in Fig. 6.2. The top part shows the inputs, extracted from the documentation provided in the case studies: requirements, BPMN models, and the approved traceability between both. The approved traceability is a document that depicts the correct fragments that correspond to the requirements. It is provided by software engineers from our industrial partner, and conforms the oracle of the evaluation.

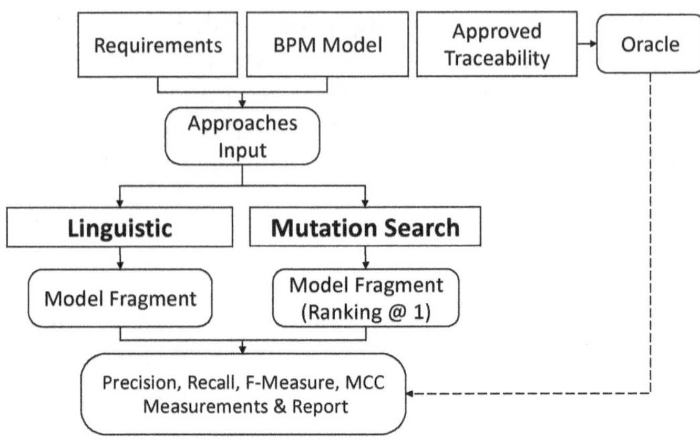

Figure 6.2: Experimental Setup

For each case study, the linguistic baseline takes the mentioned inputs, and generates a single fragment for each requirement. The generated fragment is compared with the oracle fragment. The Mutation Search technique generates a ranking of fragments per requirement instead. Since the rankings are ordered from best to worst traceability, the first fragment in each ranking is picked for comparison against its corresponding oracle. Once the comparisons are performed, a confusion matrix is calculated both for the baseline and for Mutation Search.

A confusion matrix is a table that is often used to describe the performance of a classification model (in this case, the linguistic baseline and Mutation Search) on a set of test data (the solutions) for which the true values are known (from the oracle). The confusion matrix distinguishes between the predicted values and the real values, classifying them into four categories: (1) true positive; (2) false positive; (3) true negative; and (4) false negative. Then, some performance measurements are derived from the values in the confusion matrix. In particular, a report including four performance measurements (recall, precision, f-measure, and MCC) is created for each of the two case studies, both for the baseline and for Mutation Search.

6.3.3 Case Study and Oracles

In order to perform the evaluation of the approaches, we relied on two different case studies: (1) the Camunda BPMN for Research academic repository, and (2) a set of BPMN models provided by CAF, our industrial partner. In order to obtain the performance results of the approaches, we relied on the available correct solutions, provided in both case studies.

Camunda BPMN for Research: The Camunda BPMN for Research case study consists of four BPMN modeling exercises. Each exercise contains an associated textual description and the solution model for the provided description. In order to apply the approaches to the Camunda case study, a software engineer derived a set of requirements from the problem descriptions. Each exercise has an associated solution model for the provided description. The same software engineer who derived the requirements from the problem descriptions also generated a set of fragments from the solution model, mapping each fragment to a single requirement. Thus, we were provided with a set of requirements, the fragments that implement them, and the TLR mapping between both artifacts.

CAF: For our evaluation, CAF provided us with the requirements and BPMN models of five railway solutions. They also provided us with their existing documentation on requirements to BPMN models traceability, where each requirement is also mapped to a single fragment.

6.4 Results

Table 6.1 outlines the results. Each row shows the obtained precision, recall, f-measure, and MCC values. The Mutation Search technique achieved the best results for all the performance indicators in both case studies, providing a mean precision value of 63%, a mean recall value of 77%, a combined F-measure of 68%, and an MCC value of 0.60 for the Camunda BPMN for Research case study, and a mean precision value of 79%, a mean recall value of 72%, a combined F-measure of 74%, and an MCC value of 0.69 for the CAF case study.

Table 6.1: Mean Values and Standard Deviations for Precision, Recall and F-Measure

	Precision	Recall	F-Measure	MCC
Linguistic - Camunda	40%±25%	35%±22%	33%±13%	0.25±0.19
Linguistic - CAF	35%±28%	35%±10%	30%±7%	0.18±0.13
Mutation Search - Camunda	63%±21%	77%±22%	68%±19%	0.60±0.24
Mutation Search - CAF	79%±19%	72%±19%	74%±16%	0.69±0.20

6.5 Research Question

From the results of our work, a Research Question arises: *How can we further improve TLR in BPMN models?* The following section will address this question, briefly mentioning some of the possible future works derived from a close inspection of the results.

6.6 Future Work

This section presents some ideas and opportunities for future work that arose from the presented Research Question:

1. **(Accepted - CAiSE 2019)** Tacit knowledge in the requirements may have a negative impact on semantic-based techniques. How can we minimize this impact?

2. **(Currently under review - IS CAiSE 2018 special issue)** BPMN models have some particularities that other models lack. Could we take in account these particularities in our techniques in order to lead them to enhanced results?

3. **(Ongoing work)** BMPN models have less text that other models. Could we enrich the text of BPMN models to improve TLR techniques based on text search?

6.7 Methodology

To perform this research, as well as our ongoing work, we have followed the design science methodology guidelines presented in Wieringa 2014.

6.8 Related Work

Related works focus on the impact and application of linguistic techniques to TLR problem resolution at several levels of abstraction. Works like Sultanov and Hayes 2010; Sundaram et al. 2010 use linguistic approaches to tackle specific TLR p roblems. In Falessi, C antone, and Canfora 2013, the authors use linguistic techniques to identify equivalence between requirements. The work presented in Arora et al. 2015 uses linguistic techniques to study how changes in requirements impact other requirements in the same specification. O ur work is not b ased or focused on linguistic techniques as a means of TLR analysis, but we rather study novel techniques to perform TLR between requirements and BPMN models. Other works target the application of LSI to TLR tasks. De Lucia et al. De Lucia et al. 2004 present a tool based on LSI in the context of an artifact management system. Eder et al. 2015 takes in consideration the possible configurations of LSI when using the t echnique for TLR between requirement artifacts. Through our work, we do not study the management of artifacts nor different LSI configurations or how LSI configurations impact the results of TLR, but we rather study TLR between requirements and BPMN models.

Chapter 7

Improving Traceability Links Recovery in Process Models through an Ontological Expansion of Requirements

Often, when requirements are written, parts of the domain knowledge are assumed by the domain experts and not formalized in writing, but nevertheless used to build software artifacts. This issue, known as tacit knowledge, affects the performance of Traceability Links Recovery. Through this work we propose LORE, a novel approach that uses Natural Language Processing techniques along with an Ontological Requirements Expansion process to minimize the impact of tacit knowledge on TLR over process models. We evaluated our approach through a real-world industrial case study, comparing its outcomes against those of a baseline. Results show that our approach retrieves improved results for all the measured performance indicators. We studied why this is the case, and identified some issues that affect LORE, leaving room for improvement opportunities. We make an open-source implementation of LORE publicly available in order to facilitate its adoption in future studies.

7.1 Introduction

Traceability Links Recovery (TLR) has been a subject of investigation for many years within the software engineering community (Gotel and Finkelstein 1994; Spanoudakis and Zisman 2005). Traceability can be critical to the success of a project (Watkins and Neal 1994), leads to increased maintainability and reliability of software systems (Ghazarian 2010), and decreases the expected defect rate in developed software (Rempel and Mäder 2017). However, TLR techniques rely greatly on the language of the studied documents. Often, when requirements are written, parts of the domain knowledge are not embodied in them, or embodied in ambiguous ways. This phenomena is known as tacit knowledge. The tacit knowledge is assumed by all the domain experts, and never formalized in writing. This behavior has been reported by previous works (Stone and Sawyer 2006; Arora, Sabetzadeh, Briand, et al. 2016). As a result, both the text of the requirements and the tacit knowledge are used to build software artifacts, which in turn contain elements that are related to the text of the requirement, and elements that are related to the tacit knowledge. However, since part of the knowledge is not reflected in the text of the requirement, recovering the most relevant software artifact for a requirement through TLR becomes a complex task.

Through this work, we propose LORE, a novel approach that minimizes the impact that tacit knowledge has on TLR. To that extent, Natural Language Processing (NLP) techniques are used to process the requirements, and then an ontology is used to expand the processed requirements with concepts from the domain. Finally, TLR techniques are applied to analyze the requirements and software artifacts in search for software artifact fragments that match the requirements. We have evaluated our approach by carrying out LORE between the requirements and process models that comprise a real-world industrial case study, involving the control software of the trains manufactured by our industrial partner. Results show that our approach guides TLR to enhanced results for all the measured performance indicators, providing a mean precision value of 79.2%, a mean recall value of 50.2%, a combined F-measure of 66.5%, and an MCC value of 0.62. In contrast, the baseline used for comparison presents worse results in these same measurements.

Through our work, we have also identified a series of issues related to the ontology and the requirements that prevent our approach from achieving better solutions. These issues could be tackled in the future to further improve the TLR process between requirements and process models.

Through the following pages, Section 7.2 presents the background for our work. Sections 7.3 and 7.4 provide details on our approach, and on the leveraged Traceability Links Recovery technique. Section 7.5 describes the evaluation of our approach. Section 7.6 introduces the obtained results. Section 7.7 discusses the outcomes of our work. Section 7.8 presents the threats to the validity of our work. Section 7.9 reviews works related to this one. Finally, Section 7.10 concludes the paper.

7.2   Background

In industrial scenarios, companies tend to have a myriad of products with large and complex models behind, created and maintained over long periods of time by different software engineers, who often lack knowledge over the entirety of the product details. Through this section, we provide an overview of the models in our case study, and of the problem that our approach intends to mitigate.

7.2.1   Case Study Models

Fig. 7.1 depicts one example of a model, taken from a real-world train, specified through a process model. The model has the expressiveness required to describe the interaction between the main pieces of equipment installed in a train unit, and the non-functional aspects related to regulation. Specifically, the example of the figure presents the station stop process, where a human sets the stop mode and the system opens the platform passenger doors. The elements of Fig. 7.1 highlighted in gray conform an example model fragment.

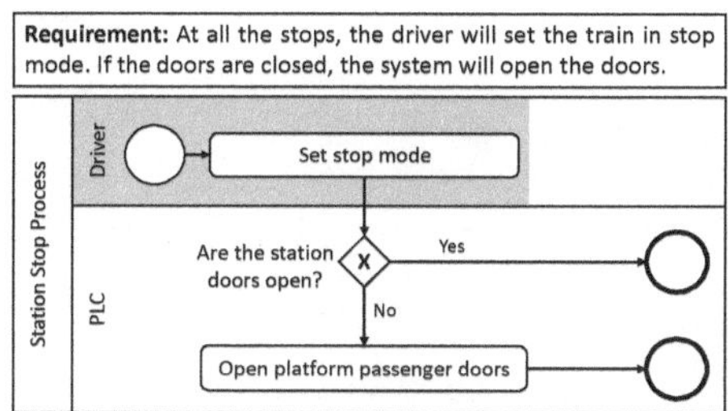

Figure 7.1: Example of Requirement, Model and Model Fragment

7.2.2 Tacit Knowledge in Requirements

However, the requirement in Fig. 7.1 is lacking important information,
known by the engineers and kept as tacit knowledge. A literal interpreta-
tion of the second sentence of the requirement implies that at all stations,
all the doors of the train will open. However, the sentence embodies tacit
knowledge that is not written but that is obvious to the domain engineers: (1) the train has doors on both sides, but only the doors on the
side of the platform will open; and (2) not all the doors will open, the
door of the control cabin will remain closed for the safety of the driver
and the train. Thus, only the platform passenger doors will open.

7.3 Our Approach

7.3.1 Approach Overview

Through the presented approach, we tackle the tacit knowledge issue presented in the prior section, by expanding requirements through a domain
ontology. The approach runs in a two-step process:

1 First, we use Natural Language Processing (NLP) techniques to process the requirement and the ontology. The NLP techniques unify
the language of the software artifacts, which facilitates the expansion process.

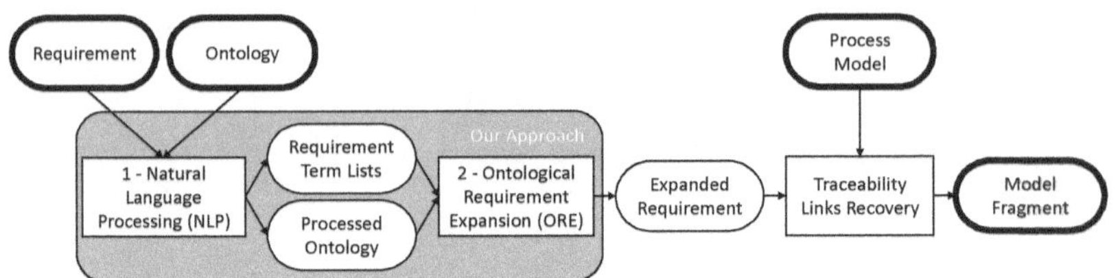

Figure 7.2: Approach Overview

2 Secondly, we propose an Ontological Requirement Expansion (ORE) process that uses the processed requirement and ontology in order to expand the requirement with related domain knowledge, diminishing the amount of tacit knowledge in the requirement.

The expanded requirement is used along with the NLP-treated process models from our case study as an input for Latent Semantic Indexing (LSI) (Landauer, Foltz, and Laham 1998), a widely accepted TLR process (Winkler and Pilgrim 2010). Through LSI, a model fragment, candidate solution for the requirement, is produced. Figure 7.2 depicts an overview of the steps of the approach. In the figure, rounded boxes represent the inputs and outputs of each step, while squared boxes represent each step. The highlighted boxes represent the initially available inputs (requirement, ontology, and model) used for the different steps of our approach and for the TLR process, and the final output (the most relevant model fragment for the requirement).

7.3.2 Natural Language Processing (NLP)

This section describes the NLP techniques taken in account for our approach. Fig. 7.3 is used to illustrate the whole compendium of techniques, detailed through the following paragraphs.

Splitting: As seen in Section 7.2, the tacit knowledge lies within the sentences of the requirements. Thus, in order to better isolate the tacit knowledge issue, we split the text of the requirements into the sentences that compose it. These smaller parts of text will help expand the requirement more accurately further on in our approach.

Fig. 7.3 depicts the two sentences that result from splitting the running example requirement.

Syntactical Analysis: Syntactical Analysis (SA) techniques analyze the specific roles of each one of them in the sentence and determine their grammatical function. These techniques (referred to as Parts-Of-Speech Tagging, or POS Tagging) allow engineers to implement filters for words that fulfill specific grammatical roles in a requirement, usually opting only for nouns (Capobianco et al. n.d.). In Fig. 7.3, it is possible to appreciate the SA process, with the POS Tagged Tokens associated to each sentence of the requirement as outcome.

Root Reduction: The technique known as Lemmatizing reduces words to their semantic roots or lemmas. Thanks to lemmas, the language of the NL requirements is unified, avoiding verb tenses, noun plurals, and other word forms that interfere negatively with the TLR process. The unification of the language semantics is an evolution over pure syntactical role filtering, allowing for a more advanced filtering of words in NL requirements. In Fig. 7.3, it is possible to appreciate the RR process, with the Root-Reduced Tokens as outcome of the semantic analysis of the POS Tags derived from the NL requirement (keeping only nouns). This process is also applied to the ontology, treating all the concepts as nouns, since domain terms always name important characteristics of the trains.

Human NLP: The inclusion of domain knowledge through experts and software engineers in the TLR process is regarded as beneficial. Human NLP is often carried out through Domain Terms Extraction or Stopwords Removal. In our approach, domain terms are checked for after splitting the requirement into sentences. We analyze each sentence in search for the domain terms provided by the software engineers, and add the found domain terms to the final processed sentence. On the other hand, stopwords are filtered out of the Root Reduced sentences. Fig. 7.3 depicts the Human NLP process, where a software engineer provides both lists of terms, which are consequently introduced into the final query, or filtered out of it.

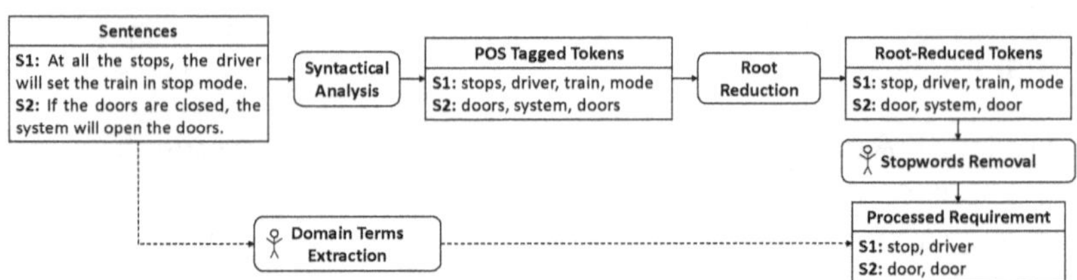

Figure 7.3: Natural Language Processing Techniques

7.3.3 Ontological Requirement Expansion (ORE)

The process that we propose in order to ontologically expand a requirement is detailed through the paragraphs of this section. The process
runs in two steps: (1) calculation of the Ontological Affinity Documents
associated to the requirement, and (2) expansion of the requirement.

1 **Ontological Affinity:** Ontological Affinity Documents (OADs) are
documents that contain a set of ontological concepts related to a
certain input. The first step of the Ontological Requirement Expansion process is to calculate the OADs associated to the requirement.
We designed an algorithm that utilizes a processed domain ontology
and a processed requirement to generate the OADs. The algorithm
first selects one of the processed sentences generated through NLP.
Then, the algorithm takes one term in the sentence, searching for
it in the ontology. If the term matches a concept that is present
in the ontology, all the concepts directly connected to the concept
are added to an OAD. The algorithm iterates over all the terms in
the sentence, generating the OAD associated to the sentence. The
process is repeated for every sentence in the processed requirement,
generating one OAD per sentence.

This process is illustrated through our running example in Fig. 7.4.
In the figure, for space reasons, only a small part of the domain
ontology is represented. In the case of the first sentence, the term
'stop' appears both in the sentence and as an ontology concept. The
concepts that are directly related to the 'stop' concept are 'station'
and 'door'.

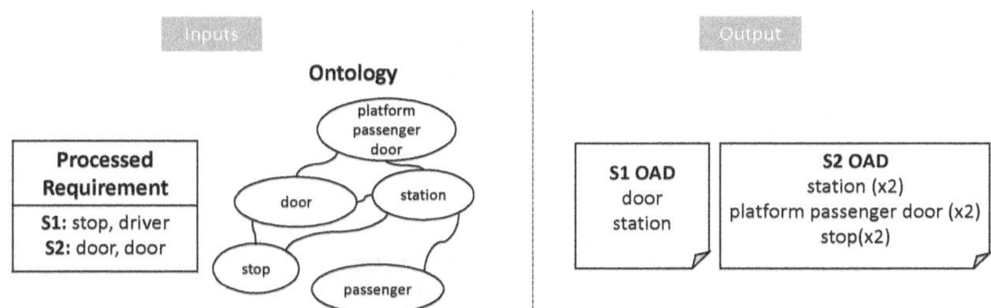

Figure 7.4: Ontological Affinity Documents Calculation

These concepts are therefore included into the OAD of the sentence. In our example, the term 'driver' does not appear as a concept in the ontology, providing no concepts for the OAD of the first sentence. In the case of the second sentence, the term 'door' appears as a concept in the example ontology. The concept is connected to 'station', 'stop', and 'platform passenger door'. Since the term appears twice in the sentence, the concepts are added twice to the OAD.

2 **Requirement Expansion:** Through this step, our approach automatically reformulates the processed requirement to expand it with terms of the OADs using a technique that is based on Rocchio's method (Salton 1971), which is perhaps the most commonly used method for query reformulation (Sisman and Kak 2013). Rocchio's method orders the terms in the OADs based on the sum of the importance of each term of the documents using the following equation:

$$Rocchio = \sum_{d \in R} TF(c, d) \cdot IDF(t, R) \tag{7.1}$$

Where R is the set of OADs, d is a document in R, and c is a concept in d. The first component of the measure is the Term Frequency (TF), which is the number of times the concept appears in a document; it is an indicator of the importance of the concept in the document compared to the rest of the concepts in that document.

The second component is the Inverse Document Frequency (IDF), which is the inverse of the number of documents that contain that concept; it indicates the specificity of that concept for a document that contains it. The IDF measurement is calculated as:

$$IDF(t, R) = \log \frac{|R|}{|\{d \in R : c \in d\}|} \tag{7.2}$$

Where $|R|$ is the number of documents and $|\{d \in R : c \in d\}|$ is the number of documents where the concept is present.

To illustrate this calculation, consider the processed requirement from our running example. After calculating the OADs presented in Fig. 7.4, Rocchio's method is applied to the concepts of the documents in order to retrieve the importance of said concepts. Take in account the concept 'platform passenger door'. In the first document, the concept does not appear ($TF = 0$), immediately leading to a $TF \cdot IDF$ value of $TF \cdot IDF = 0$. The concept appears twice in the second document ($TF = 2$) and appears in one of two documents ($IDF = \log \frac{2}{1} \approx 0.3$), which leads to a $TF \cdot IDF$ value of $TF \cdot IDF \approx 0.6$. The sum of both $TF \cdot IDF$ values leads to a total *Rocchio* value of *Rocchio* ≈ 0.6. Using Rocchio's method, the concepts of the OADs associated to the sentences of the requirement are ordered from highest to lowest sum of importance into a single document of concepts. Once ordered, we take in consideration only the first 10 suggestions and discard the rest, as is recommended in the literature (Carpineto and Romano 2012). The list of the 10 first suggested concepts conforms the OAD associated to the requirement.

Since the objective of our approach is to mitigate the tacit knowledge of the requirement, our aim is to find new domain knowledge to include in the requirement, and therefore we refine the requirement OAD by discarding those concepts in the OAD that already appear in any sentence of the requirement.

In our running example, this process would produce a requirement OAD consisting of the terms 'station' and 'platform passenger door', since both 'door' and 'stop' are already present in the sentences of the requirement. The terms of the processed sentences and the concepts on the refined OAD are then concatenated into a single list of terms. This final list of terms is the ultimate goal that our approach seeks to obtain: an expanded requirement, enriched with ontological domain knowledge. The expanded requirement is the final output of the Ontological Requirement Expansion process, and is used as query for the Traceability Links Recovery process.

7.4 Traceability Links Recovery

LORE can be applied to any TLR technique that uses a requirement as input. Through this work, we utilize Latent Semantic Indexing (LSI), the TLR technique that obtains the best results when performing TLR between requirements and software artifacts (Winkler and Pilgrim 2010). Latent Semantic Indexing (LSI) (Landauer, Foltz, and Laham 1998) constructs vector representations of a query and a corpus of text documents by encoding them as a *term-by-document co-occurrence matrix*. In our approach, *terms* are each of the words that compose the expanded requirement and NL representation of the input model (extracted through the technique presented in (Meziane, Athanasakis, and Ananiadou n.d.)), *documents* are the model elements in the input model, and the *query* is the expanded requirement. Each cell in the matrix contains the frequency with which the *term* of its row appears in the *document* denoted by its column. Once the matrix is built, it is normalized and decomposed into a set of vectors using a matrix factorization technique called Singular Value Decomposition (SVD) (Landauer, Foltz, and Laham 1998).

The similarity degree between the query and each document is calculated through the cosine between the vectors that represent them. Fig. 7.5 shows an example matrix, built from our running example, the result of applying the SVD technique to the matrix, and the resulting scores associated to each document.

		Documents			Query
		ME1	**ME2**	**...**	**MEN**	**Requirement**
Keywords	PLC	0	0	...	0	0
	platform passenger door	0	1	...	0	1
	door	0	1	...	1	2
	...	...	...	...	...	...

Singular Value Decomposition

Scores

Model Fragment Similitude Scores
ME2 = 0.93
MEN = 0.85
...
ME1 = -0.87

Figure 7.5: Traceability Link Recovery through Latent Semantic Indexing Example

In our approach, we use the top ranked model elements to build a model fragment that serves as a candidate for realizing the requirement. Of all the model elements, only those that have a similarity measure greater than x must be taken into account. A widely used heuristic is $x = 0.7$. This value corresponds to a 45° angle between the corresponding vectors. Even though the selection of the threshold is an issue under study, the chosen heuristic has yielded good results in other similar works (Marcus et al. 2004; Salman, Seriai, and Dony 2014).

7.5 Evaluation

This section presents the evaluation of our approach, including the experimental setup, a description of the case study where we applied the evaluation, and the implementation details of our approach.

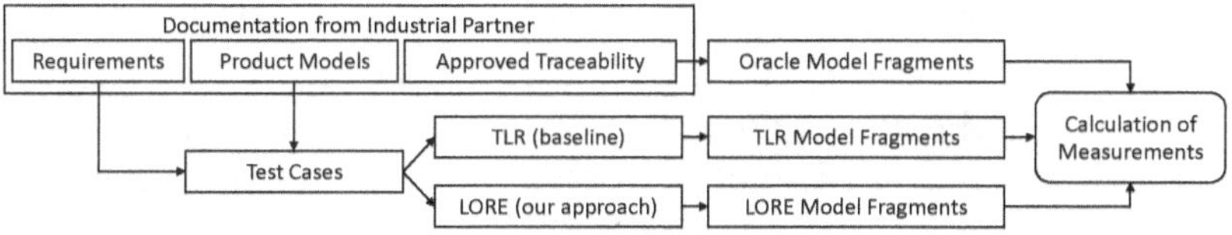

Figure 7.6: Experimental Setup

7.5.1 Experimental Setup

The goal of this experiment is to perform TLR between requirements and models through LORE, comparing its results against the baseline. The baseline against which we compare our work is the technique that obtains the best results when recovering Traceability between requirements and models according to the literature, TLR through LSI. The baseline utilizes the processed requirement, without performing the ontological expansion in use in LORE. Fig. 7.6 shows an overview of the process followed to evaluate our approach (LORE) and the baseline (TLR). The top part of the figure shows the inputs, as provided by our industrial partner. The requirements and models are used to build the test cases (one requirement and one model each) and the approved Traceability is used to build the oracles against which the results of the approaches are compared.

For each test case, both LORE and TLR generate one model fragment each. The model fragments generated for each test case are compared against their respective oracles (ground truth), and a confusion matrix is calculated for each of the two approaches. A confusion matrix is a table used to describe the performance of a classification model on a set of test data for which the true values are known. In our case, the presence or absence of each model element is considered as a classification. The confusion matrix arranges the results of the classifications into four categories: (1) True Positive (predicted true, true in the real scenario), (2) False Positive (predicted true, false in the real scenario), (3) True Negative (predicted false, false in the real scenario), and (4) False Negative (predicted false, true in the real scenario). From the confusion matrix, it is possible to extract some measurements that evaluate the performance of the approach.

We report four performance measurements for both LORE and TLR: Recall, Precision, F-measure, and MCC (Matthews Correlation Coefficient). Recall measures the number of elements of the solution that are correctly retrieved by the proposed solution, precision measures the number of elements from the solution that are correct according to the ground truth, and the F-measure corresponds to the harmonic mean of precision and recall. The MCC is a correlation coefficient between the observed and predicted binary classifications (Salton and McGill 1986; Marcus et al. 2004).

Recall values can range between 0% (no single model element from the oracle is present in the retrieved model fragment) to 100% (all the model elements from the oracle are present in the retrieved model fragment). Precision values can range between 0% (no model elements from the retrieved model fragment appear in the oracle) to 100% (all the model elements from the retrieved model fragment appear in the oracle). MCC values can range between -1 (no correlation between the prediction and the oracle) to 1 (perfect prediction). Moreover, an MCC value of 0 corresponds to a random prediction.

7.5.2 Case Study

The case study where we applied our approach was provided by our industrial partner, CAF (`http://www.caf.es/en`), a worldwide provider of railway solutions. Our evaluation includes 140 test cases, with each test case comprising one requirement, one model, and the approved Traceability between the requirement and the model. The requirements have about 25 words on average, and the models are formed through 650 elements on average. For each test case, we followed the experimental setup described in Figure 7.6.

Regarding the domain ontology in use, it comprises 27 concepts and 176 relationships. The construction of an ontology is a major effort which requires the study of the domain structure and terminology. We did not try to address the creation of a new ontology in this paper but instead, our industrial partner provided us with the ontology they use for training new employees.

The ontology is an important artifact and its quality, size, and completeness may have an impact on the results. In a future work, we intend to analyze the extent of this impact on the results of LORE.

7.5.3 Implementation details

For the development of the Natural Language Processing operations used in both our approach and the baseline, we have used the OpenNLP Toolkit (Apache 2016). To implement the LSI and SVD techniques, the Efficient Java Matrix Library (EJML) was used (Abeles n.d.). For the evaluation, we used a Lenovo E330 laptop, with a processor Intel(R) Core(TM) i5-3210M@2.5GHz with 16GB RAM and Windows 10 (64-bit). A prototype of LORE can be found at `bitbucket.org/svitusj/lore`.

7.6 Results

Table 7.1 outlines the results of the TLR baseline and our LORE approach. Each row shows the Precision, Recall, F-measure, and MCC values obtained through each of the two approaches. The LORE approach achieves the best results for all the performance indicators, providing a mean precision value of 79.2%, a mean recall value of 50.2%, a combined F-measure of 66.5%, and an MCC value of 0.62. In contrast, the TLR baseline presents worse results in all the measurements, attaining a mean precision value of 59.3%, a mean recall value of 45.5%, a combined F-measure of 52.4%, and an MCC value of 0.31. We also included the values of the measurements for the top 20 and the bottom 20 results for TLR and LORE, to better highlight how the results obtained by LORE improve those obtained by the TLR baseline.

7.7 Discussion

The results presented in the previous section suggest that by embedding domain knowledge into requirements the TLR process retrieves enhanced results. Taking a closer look at the test cases, we found out that there are many terms in the models that do not appear in the requirements.

Table 7.1: Mean Values and Standard Deviations for Precision, Recall and F-Measure

	Precision	Recall	F-Measure	MCC
TLR	59.3%±29.6%	45.5%±34.2%	52.4%±31.9%	0.31±0.13
LORE	79.2%±33.6%	50.2%±30.6%	66.5%±38.6%	0.62±0.32
Top 20 - TLR	81.3%±7.3%	55.4%±3.2%	68.3%±5.2%	0.41±0.03
Top 20 - LORE	93.4%±8.4%	69.8%±4.6%	81.6%±6.5%	0.86±0.04
Bottom 20 - TLR	48.3%±6.9%	19.8%±4.2%	34.1%±5.5%	0.22±0.04
Bottom 20 - LORE	66.2%±5.7%	41.2%±5.1%	53.7%±5.4%	0.38±0.08

Through the ontological expansion of the requirements, they are enriched with otherwise missing terms, retrieving more and better links. However, we also noticed a series of facts that prevent LORE from achieving better results than it does. We should tackle these issues in the future to further improve our line of work:

1 Our analysis of the results raised awareness about the importance of the quality and completeness of the ontology in LORE. If a particular concept does not have quality connections, the quality of the expansion process is diminished, also affecting the quality of the final outcome. Equally, if a concept is missing from the ontology, the concept itself and its would-be related concepts cannot be introduced in the expanded requirement. This issue leaves parts of the domain knowledge out from the requirement, causing a decrease in recall. In order to tackle this issue, we plan to automatically identify words and patterns of words that occur repeatedly in the requirements and models, and suggest their inclusion in the ontology as concepts, entrusting the creation of their relationships to the software engineers.

2 In the ontology, we identified some terms that have a large number of connections to other terms. Matching one of those terms through LORE leads to the inclusion of several unwanted ontological concepts into the expanded requirement. This concatenation of events reflects into LSI noise, strongly affecting in a negative manner the precision of the results, since elements that are not part of the oracle can be added to the proposed solution due to this issue.

To tackle this issue, we plan to automatically identify the overly connected ontological concepts and suggest their inclusion in the stopwords list to the software engineers, so they can be kept out of the LORE analysis.

3 Another possible consideration towards the obtained results is the parameter tuning of our approach. Many Information Retrieval approaches have parameters that can be tuned in order to improve the results (such as the LSI similitude threshold), and our approach is no exception. So far, we have considered only the directly related ontological concepts when performing the expansion (one jump or ontological affinity level 1). In the future, we plan to study how using different levels of affinity may impact the results. We believe this could help us further explore the ontology and the relationships between the concepts, although at a risk of including noise into LSI. Analyzing the tuning of this parameter and its implications and impact on the outcomes of the LORE approach remains as future work.

4 Regarding recall, we have inspected the results and have determined that the low recall levels are not dependent solely on the techniques under use, but are also affected by the quality of the received queries, which in several occasions, are poorly formulated. Focusing only on these particular cases, recall values obtained by TLR range at 20%, while recall values obtained by LORE range at 40%. However, for better quality queries, TLR recall results range at 55%, while those of LORE range at 70%. The point is, considering ontological knowledge in the process helps improve traceability results. That is, in the face of poor quality inputs, the results improve, but if we feed LORE with better queries, the results improve as well. Studying the quality of the inputs and how to ensure it remains as an interesting research topic for a future work in which we might as well design another experiment to research how LORE improves the results of TLR for top-quality queries.

In any case, as a naive experiment and in order to ensure the usefulness of the obtained results, we have discussed them with one of the software engineers working for our industrial partner, who has confirmed that the model fragments obtained by LORE serve as a better starting point for requirement-model tracing than those obtained by plain TLR.

5 Finally, in many cases, different terms are used to reference the same concept in the requirements, models, and ontology alike. In industrial environments, the engineers in charge of writing requirements may not be assigned with the building of the models or the ontology in any ways, being those tasks left for different engineers. Moreover, the artifacts can be manipulated by different engineers. This issue is known as vocabulary mismatch. Even though LORE uses NLP to homogenize the language between requirements and models, the vocabulary mismatch continues to be a disregarded issue in our work. The lack of awareness caused by the vocabulary mismatch makes it impossible to locate the elements from the model that are relevant to the requirement, which in turn negatively impacts both precision and recall. To mitigate this issue, we plan on adding a third human-made list, comprising in-house terms and their possible synonyms, allowing us to further map ontology concepts and requirements.

7.8 Threats to validity

In this section, we use the classification of threats to validity of (Wohlin et al. 2012) to acknowledge the limitations of our approach.

1 **Construct validity:** This aspect of validity reflects the extent to which the operational measures that are studied represent what the researchers have in mind. To minimize this risk, our evaluation studies four measures that are widely accepted in the software engineering research community: precision, recall, F-measure, and MCC.

2 Internal Validity: This aspect of validity is of concern when causal relations are examined. There is a risk that the factor being investigated may be affected by other neglected factors. The number of requirements and models presented in this work may look small, but they implement a wide scope of different railway equipment.

3 External Validity: This aspect of validity is concerned with to what extent it is possible to generalize the findings, and to what extent the findings are of relevance for other cases. Both requirements and process models are frequently leveraged to specify all kinds of different software. LSI is a widely accepted and utilized technique which has proven to obtain good results in multiple domains. The NLP techniques studied through this work are also commonly used in the whole of the SE community. Therefore, our experiment does not rely on the particular conditions of our domain. In addition, the real-world models used in our research are a good representative of the railway, automotive, aviation, and general industrial manufacturing domains. Nevertheless, the experiment and its results should be replicated in other domains before assuring their generalization.

4 Reliability: This aspect is concerned with to what extent the data and the analysis are dependent on the specific researchers. To reduce this threat, all the software artifacts were provided by our industrial partner.

7.9   Related Work

Some works focus on the impact and application of Linguistics to TLR at several levels of abstraction. Works like (Sultanov and Hayes 2010; Sundaram et al. 2010) or (Duan and Cleland-Huang 2007) use Linguistic approaches to tackle specific TLR problems and tasks. In (Falessi, Cantone, and Canfora 2013), the authors use Linguistic techniques to identify equivalence between requirements, also defining and using a series of principles for evaluating their performance when identifying equivalent requirements.

The authors of (Falessi, Cantone, and Canfora 2013) conclude that, in their field, the performance of Linguistic techniques is determined by the properties of the given dataset over which they are performed. They measure the properties as a factor to adjust the Linguistic techniques accordingly, and then apply their principles to an industrial case study. The work presented in (Arora, Sabetzadeh, Goknil, et al. 2015) uses Linguistic techniques to study how changes in requirements impact other requirements in the same specification. Through the pages of their work, the authors analyze TLR between requirements, and use Linguistic techniques to determine how changes in requirements must propagate.

Our work differs from (Sultanov and Hayes 2010; Sundaram et al. 2010) and (Duan and Cleland-Huang 2007) since our approach is not based on Linguistic techniques as a means of TLR, but we rather use an ontological expansion process to enrich requirements before performing TLR, using NLP techniques only as a preprocess in our work. Moreover, we do not study how Linguistic techniques must be tweaked for specific problems as (Falessi, Cantone, and Canfora 2013) does. In addition, differing from (Arora, Sabetzadeh, Goknil, et al. 2015), we do not tackle changes in requirements nor TLR between requirements, but instead focus our work on TLR between requirements and models.

Other works target the application of LSI to TLR tasks. De Lucia et al. (De Lucia et al. 2004) present a Traceability Links Recovery method and tool based on LSI in the context of an artifact management system, which includes models. (Eder et al. 2015) takes in consideration the possible configurations of LSI when using the technique for TLR between requirements artifacts, namely requirements and test cases. In their work, the authors state that the configurations of LSI depend on the datasets used, and they look forward to automatically determining an appropriate configuration for LSI for any given dataset. Through our work, we do not focus on the usage of LSI or its tuning, but rather expand requirements with ontological domain knowledge before carrying out TLR between said requirements and the models.

7.10 Conclusions

Through this work, we propose a novel approach (LORE), based on an Ontological Requirement Expansion process, that can be used to minimize the impact that tacit knowledge has on TLR. We evaluated our approach by carrying out LORE between the requirements and process models that comprise a real-world industrial case study. Results show that our approach guides TLR to the best results for all the measured performance indicators, providing a mean precision value of 79.2%, a mean recall value of 50.2%, a combined F-measure of 66.5%, and an MCC value of 0.62. In contrast, the baseline used for comparison presents worse results in these same measurements. In addition, we identified a series of issues that prevent our approach from achieving better solutions, and that should be tackled in the future in order to further improve the TLR process between requirements and process models. To facilitate the adoption of LORE, we made a reference implementation freely available for the Eclipse environment.

Part III

Discussion

Discussion

Through the pages of this chapter, we discuss the rationale for the development of the thesis. We also discuss the results of our work by connecting the research questions posed at the start of the thesis with the research articles that conform the compendium included in chapters 1 to 7. In addition, we describe our ongoing research and the ideas for future works.

Thesis Development Rationale

Before the start of the thesis, through the experiences and expertise of other authors in the same research environment, and through a thorough study of the available literature, we came to know of Traceability Links Recovery and its importance within the Software Engineering community.

However, we could also identify a shortcoming with regards to the available research on the topic within artifacts other than code. In particular, we identified a lack of research with regards to model-based software artifacts in general, and more specifically, within the context of BPMN models.

Therefore, our first efforts were aimed at transforming the state-of-the-art approaches in code-based software artifacts, so that they could be transported to model-based software artifacts. We published this work in CAiSE Forum 2017, chapter 1, which served as an approximation to the research world and community, and as a great learning experience in terms of presentation and networking.

While our initial work was substantially successful, we identified a series of problems related to the natural language of the artifacts in use. In particular, we had some issues that stemmed from the transformation of models to natural language (a necessary step for the application of the developed Traceability Links Recovery approaches), and from the processing of the natural language in the requirements.

We deliberated on whether to tackle both issues at once or to do so separately. We came to the conclusion that isolating the problems would help reduce the costs and risks of development, and that it would also help explain the issues themselves and the obtained results in written research. In addition, we wanted to explore how each of the issues was affecting the context problem. Hence, in the end, we decided to deal with those issues one at a time. These studies were embodied into two research papers for ER Forum 2017, chapter 2, and GPCE 2017 (GGS class 3, CORE:B), chapter 3.

These two experiences confirmed the adequacy of the direction of the research, and contributed to the development of very valuable research skills, leading to improvements in written expression and structuring and presentation of information.

At this point, we recapped our work, integrating the latest research improvements to the Traceability Links Recovery approaches that we first developed. At the same point of time, an opportunity arose for incorporating the novel enhancements to the research that stemmed from the work of other authors in the same research environment in the fields of Feature Location and Bug Location, two other Software Engineering tasks that pursue different goals than those of Traceability Links Recovery, but which still rely on Information Retrieval to do so. The results of this research, to which the Traceability Links Recovery component was provided by the work achieved as part of this thesis, were published in 2018 in an article for volume 103 of the Information and Software Technology Journal (2nd quartile in its category), chapter 4 of this thesis. This particular research experience improved other valuable skills, such as teamwork in research, or understanding the differences between conferences and journals and the involved research processes.

Afterwards, we knew it was time to leave the generalist level of model-based software artifacts, and dive into the specifics of BPMN models. To that extent, we applied our newfound knowledge to develop an approach for Traceability Links Recovery in the BPMN models context. The results of this work were published in CAiSE 2018 (GGS class 2, CORE:A), chapter 5 of this thesis. This work not only shaped the remainder of the thesis, but also provided a certain degree of visibility and very valuable feedback from the research community.

However, as it had occurred at the beginning of the thesis, we identified a set of issues and problems that were negatively impacting the developed approaches, this time due to the particularities inherent to the BPMN models context. In particular, we were able to identify that the requirements in use tend to present high levels of tacit knowledge, and that BPMN models contain very little text (and in turn a very small amount of language payload) when compared to other software artifacts, including other model-based software artifacts.

We also identified a set of BPMN model particularities that could be leveraged to lead the approaches to enhanced results. We reflected on these issues in a paper for the CAiSE PhD Consortium 2019, chapter 6 of this thesis, which helped us to gather more feedback from the community, and to address the future directions of our work.

However, prior to the publication of the aforementioned CAiSE 2019 PhD Consortium paper, we were already deliberating on the identified issues and which one to tackle. We recalled that one of the authors in the research environment had been working towards requirement expansion techniques for her own research challenges, and realized that it was possible to adapt those techniques and leverage them to build a requirement expansion approach based on a domain ontology, which would help us bridge the gap between the artifacts. We developed this work and published the results in another article in the main track of CAiSE 2019 (GGS class 2, CORE:A). This particular work honed and matured the prior skills taught by previous experiences.

In the final stages of the thesis, I participated in a research stay program within another research entity (LIP6, Paris) under the tutelage of Prof. Dr. Tewfik Ziadi. There, we developed several ideas and built bridges for working together in the near future. This international experience helped me understand how other research environments organize and function, and the similarities and differences for international PhD programs and students around the world.

Finally, I built this book, and commenced working towards the rest of the ideas and issues exposed by my previous research.

Research Questions

The two research questions posed at the introduction of this thesis have been tackled throughout the research works presented in chapters 1 to 7. In the following paragraphs, we present how each of the research articles has contributed to the study of the research questions:

RQ1 Is it possible to adapt state-of-the-art Information Retrieval approaches in order to make them available for Traceability Links Recovery between natural language requirements and BPMN models?

> **CAiSE Forum '17, chapter 1** : This article is focused on transforming state-of-the-art Traceability Links Recovery techniques so that they can be leveraged for the context of requirements and generic model artifacts.

> **IST '18, chapter 4** : This article is aimed at retrieving the most relevant model fragments for different types of input queries, coming from three different Software Engineering tasks: Traceability Links Recovery, Bug Location and Feature Location. As a part of this thesis, we fully developed the part of this work that delves on Traceability Links Recovery.

> **CAiSE '18, chapter 5** : This article takes the techniques for Traceability Links Recovery between requirements and models, plus the enhancements proposed in other works in this thesis, and builds an approach for Traceability Links Recovery between requirements and BPMN models.

Response to RQ1 : The results of the aforementioned papers propose approaches for Traceability Links Recovery between requirements and BPMN models, through the adaption of existing techniques that worked for Traceability Links Recovery between requirements and code-based artifacts. In addition, the results of both articles prove, with the usage of measurements widely accepted by the scientific Software Engineering community, that these approaches and techniques can be successfully adapted for the context under study.

RQ2 If so, how can we refine the proposed approaches in order to improve the Traceability Links Recovery process between natural language requirements and BPMN models?

> **ER Forum '17, chapter 2** : This article studies the process of transforming the models into natural language with the aim of improving the Traceability Links Recovery process.

GPCE '17, chapter 3 : This article studies the processing of the natural language of the artifacts in use, with the aim of achieving further improvements on the Traceability Links Recovery process.

CAiSE PhD Consortium '19, chapter 6 : This article recaps the Traceability Links Recovery process between requirements and BPMN models, and theorizes on potential further improvements of the process.

CAiSE '19, chapter 7 : This article builds on the ideas presented by the prior paper, and enhances the Traceability Links Recovery process by palliating tacit knowledge in requirements, expanding them through the usage of a domain ontology.

Response to RQ2 : The results of the aforementioned papers tackle diverse aspects of the artifacts in use, identifying particularities of the requirements, the models, and the natural language in use alike. The possibilities posed by the inherent flaws of the artifacts are leveraged to build enhanced approaches for Traceability Links Recovery between requirements and BPMN models.

By acknowledging and incorporating these particularities, the approaches are better equipped to deal with the challenge under study, and thus obtain better results, again in terms of widely accepted measurements, than those baseline approaches that do not take in account this novel knowledge. Hence, our research proves that these approaches and techniques can be successfully refined to improve the task under study.

Future Work

This section presents some of the ideas and opportunities for future work that arose from our latest research:

1. Through a thorough analysis of the results of our work, we have identified a set of particularities of BPMN models, or in other words, a set of characteristics that differentiate BPMN models from other kinds of models, and which may be negatively affecting the Traceability Links Recovery process. Thus, a novel research question arises: *Could we take in account these particularities in the developed approaches in order to lead them to enhanced results?*

   To that extent, it would be necessary to devise mechanisms for incorporating those particularities into the developed approaches, and to analyze the impact of the novel approaches to check whether acknowledging these particularities leads the approaches to significantly enhanced results.

2. Through an analysis of the artifacts, we have realized that BMPN models have less text that other kinds of models, in particular those models that are built with code generation purposes in mind. The following research question arises: *Would it be possible to enrich the text of BPMN models to improve TLR techniques based on text search?*

   To that extent, it would be necessary to devise a mechanism that allowed us to expand the BPMN models, perhaps by leveraging other software artifacts that we have not taken into consideration so far, such as BPMN run-time execution traces, which may contain relevant information about the models, and which could be utilized to expand the amount of natural language in the BPMN models prior to performing the Traceability Links Recovery process.

These ideas constitute the seed for a yet uncharted but clear path towards future improvements, and allow us to keep working in a topic that is still an open, interesting, and relevant issue for the Software Engineering community.

Part IV

Conclusions

Conclusions

This chapter presents the final concluding remarks of the thesis, summarizing the challenge, scope, and outcomes of our work.

Traceability Links Recovery (TLR) is defined as the software engineering task that deals with the identification and comprehension of dependencies and relationships between software artifacts. It is an important support activity during activities related to development, management, and maintenance of software, leading to increased maintainability and reliability of software systems, and decreasing the expected defect rate in developed software. However, establishing and maintain traceability links has proven to be a time consuming, error prone, and person-power intensive task, and has therefore become a subject of investigation for many years within the software engineering community. However, the application of TLR techniques to models in general, and BPMN models in particular, is a topic that has not received enough attention yet.

Through this thesis, we have analyzed and improved the TLR process between natural language requirements and BPMN models. To that extent:

1. In the first stages of the thesis, our first efforts were aimed at transforming the state-of-the-art approaches in code-based software artifacts, so that they could be transported to model-based software artifacts.

2. As a result of our initial work, we identified a series of problems related to the natural language of the artifacts in use. In particular, we had some issues that stemmed from the transformation of models to natural language (a necessary step for the application of the developed Traceability Links Recovery approaches), and from the processing of the natural language in the requirements. We studied these particularities and how to leverage them to enhance the Traceability Links Recovery process.

3. Afterwards, we incorporated the novel enhancements to the research that stemmed from the work of other authors in the same research environment in the fields of Feature Location and Bug Location, two other Software Engineering tasks that pursue different goals than those of Traceability Links Recovery, but which still rely on Information Retrieval to do so.

4. Then, we dived into the specifics of BPMN models by applying our newfound knowledge to develop an approach for Traceability Links Recovery in the BPMN models context, and identified certain particularities of the research challenge in the context.

5. In the final stages of the book, we worked towards towards incorporating the particularities of the BPMN models case into the TLR approaches, improving the results of the approaches and studying potential future works in the field.

Our research has been validated through real-world case studies, both industrial and academical. In addition, our research has contributed to several national and international projects. Partial results of our research have been published in several scientific articles in workshops and conferences, relevant in the field of our studies. Overall, the results of our research have concluded that: (1) it is possible to design approaches that perform TLR between natural language requirements and BPMN models, and (2) approaches for TLR between natural language requirements and BPMN models can be enhanced, although many improvements are yet to be researched. This uncharted territory leaves room for future work in such an interesting and relevant topic.

To close this book, we reflect that, while there is still much work to do in the field, we have conclusively developed a PhD book that successfully contributes to advancing the available research knowledge in Traceability Links Recovery in BPMN models.